PRAISE

MW01075862

Joel is on a mission to usher in
ing, and with *Awake*, we have been given a chance to go along for the ride.
His inventive use of multimedia gives the reader a one-of-a-kind opportunity to dive deeper into his vibrantly told stories from his travels around the
world. Take this journey of story with Joel. You will be glad you did.

Matthew West, Contemporary Christian Music singer/songwriter

Awake is breaking new ground both in its integration of new technology and
in Joel's invitation to us to wake up and join together in God's Story. Joel is
a captivating storyteller who had me tearing through the pages to see what
happens next in his journey.

Tim Beatty, executive director of Christ Church, Fairfax Station, Virginia

Joel Clark's book *Awake* gives new meaning to the scriptural promise that
"perfect love casts out fear." It is a compelling description of God's invitation
to each of us to live boldly, to have the courage to be fully present to the
glory and tragedy that surrounds us in each moment, and to embrace the
opportunities to make a difference for good even in the most dangerous and
unexpected situations.

Shirley Mullen, president of Houghton College, Houghton, New York

Joel masterfully tells the story—his, yours, and mine. His writing stirs the
reader to dream. His wild adventures awaken a hunger to have our own.
Inspired, humorous, and packed with revelation, *Awake* is just what the title
promises, a full-on invitation to dream, love, and live our own story—a
story that can change the world. If you read one book this year, read the one
by Joel's older and arguably better-looking brother, Jason Clark. But if you
decide to read another, I highly recommend this one!

Jason Clark, author of Surrendered and Untamed: A Field Guide
for the Vagabond Believer

Awake grabs the very core of your being. The desire to awaken to one's dreams rises with the powerful storytelling of Joel and Jesus. The captivating principles subtlety move one's spirit and sinew to courageous action. Imagine how our world would flourish if every reader became AWAKE! This would be the pleasure of God realized.

> *Jo Anne Lyon, founder of World Hope International and*
> *general superintendent of the Wesleyan Church*

From the midst of the raucous, chilling, glory-strewn, and hazardous events of his life and profession, Joel calls out and points us to the God who yearns for us fully awaken and respond to child slavery, kidnappings, HIV/AIDS, and the gift of profound human love.

> *Evvy Hay Campbell, PhD, board chair of World Hope International*

Jason Bourne and John Rambo, your lives are boring. Joel Nykyforchyn-Clark, is crashing through a life that's beyond crazy, and he's driven not by a movie director but by a passionate faith in the Inventor of adventure. In this page-turner, Clark tells of how he adopted years ago the life motto "Do it for the story" and shares how it has led him to crisscross the planet ever since, looking for the newest adventure to test his wits, exhaust his energy, and scare him—and us—to death. Can't wait for the movie version to come out—but it will take someone gutsier than Matt Damon or Sylvester Stallone to play the lead role.

> *Jack Haberer, author of* GodViews: The Convictions that Drive Us
> and Divide Us

AWAKE

DISCOVER THE POWER OF **YOUR** STORY

AWAKE

THE BOOK YOU CAN WATCH

JOEL N. **CLARK**

ZONDERVAN®

ZONDERVAN.com/
AUTHORTRACKER
follow your favorite authors

ZONDERVAN

Awake
Copyright © 2012 by Joel Nykyforchyn-Clark

This title is also available as a Zondervan ebook.
Visit www.zondervan.com/ebooks.

Requests for information should be addressed to:
Zondervan, *Grand Rapids, Michigan 49530*

Library of Congress Cataloging-in-Publication Data
Clark, Joel N., 1976-
    Awake : discover the power of your story / Joel N. Clark.
      p. cm.
    ISBN 978-0-310-33465-1 (softcover)
     1. Christian life. 2. Clark, Joel N., 1976- I. Title.
    BV4501.3.C524 2012
    248.4—dc23   2011050005

Published in association with the literary agency of Fedd & Company, Inc., Post Office Box 341973, Austin, TX 78734.

Cover design: Curt Diepenhorst
Cover photography: Joel N. Clark
Interior photography: Joel N. Clark
Interior illustrations: Mike Cody, Heidi Tungseth, and Holly Sharp
Interior design: SharpSeven Design

Printed in the United States of America

12 13 14 15 16 /DCI/ 20 19 18 17 16 15 14 13 12 11 10 9 8 7 6 5 4 3 2 1

Megan,
you bring beauty, magic, and whimsy into my life.
I love that we live in a musical —
for where there is music,
laughter and dancing will always be found.
My heart is yours, now and forever.

CONTENTS

FOREWORD
by Mark Batterson

I first met Joel N. Clark back in 2008. He called me up and asked if I would be interested in working with him on a project. Joel had just returned home from a month of filming in Antarctica and wanted to show me what he had created while there. Intrigued, I met him for coffee. It was in this first meeting that I began to understand that Joel views life from a different perspective than most people do; he filters everything through the eye of Story.

After watching his Antarctic adventure, I immediately signed on to the project. Who wouldn't have? It was brilliant! Over the years, we have worked together on several projects and met for many more coffees. Although I feel like I know him pretty well, it wasn't until I read this book that I truly began to understand him. Within these pages are enough adventures to fill ten lifetimes. Whether he's running from the secret police in China, hiding from UN tanks while spending days with Haiti's top gang leaders, bungee jumping off a Johannesburg skyscraper, interviewing child slaves for a documentary, or chasing the girl of his dreams all over the world, Joel awakens a desire for adventure in even the tamest souls.

Yet Joel isn't an adrenaline junky, and he definitely has both feet firmly planted on the ground. In every story, even in those that might otherwise feel unimportant, he somehow manages to transform the seemingly mundane into a meaningful adventure. And this, according to Joel, is the power of story. When we choose to live a story that is greater than us, we find God in the midst of it. These stories take him beyond the walls of the church into places around the world where Jesus is inviting his followers to make a difference.

More than a montage of well-told stories, *Awake* is a call to action. From the very first page, you will be swept into an adventure that will have you laughing, crying, or feeling as though you've been punched in the gut. Each story will inspire you to live a greater story of your own, to love more fully and experience God more intimately. Think *carpe diem* with teeth.

What I love about this book is that Joel doesn't try to teach us how to live a better story. He doesn't give us the dynamics of story, a list of "how-tos," or rules for better living. Rather, he shows us what it means to live life to the fullest. In these pages, I experienced the truth of what it means to find God in the midst of my own story. I may not hang out with gangsters in Haiti, but the truth I found within this story is still relevant to my life. Joel doesn't spell out what a given story should mean to you or me; he tells what it means to him and invites us to experience our own stories within these pages. And this is the real power of *Awake*. Rather than preaching a message that stirs the head, he presents a story that moves the heart.

You will notice that I have yet to mention Joel's revolutionary new format. *Awake* is interactive in a way that will take your breath away. The format is amazing—a game changer, in fact. The films, art, and websites embedded in *Awake* are unlike anything that currently exists. Each entry is itself a story, an experience on its own. For example, the films allow you to actually meet the people and experience the places contained within these pages as well as many other adventures that didn't make it into the book.

Before you begin this adventure, I will only tell you this—hold on. Don't simply get excited about the stories told within these pages, but ask God to speak through them. Pray that you'll not only find God in the midst of Joel's stories but that you'll also see him at work in every aspect of your own story as well.

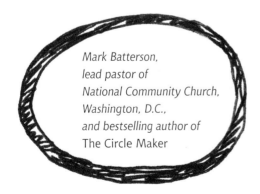

Mark Batterson,
lead pastor of
National Community Church,
Washington, D.C.,
and bestselling author of
The Circle Maker

A NOTE TO THE READER

Welcome to the adventure of *Awake!* You are about to embark on a new experience. This book is a first of its kind, and sometimes we need a map to navigate uncharted waters. Perhaps you are already QR code savvy. If so, skip this page and dive in. If, like most folks, you look at that funny square code and wonder what it's all about, read below, and get ready for an exciting adventure.

Simple to Use

A QR code is a mobile bar code that is embedded with content that smartphone users can easily access. Just download the QR code reader app of your choice (there are many free ones available), scan the codes, and engage with the page. There are even some places in the book for you to lay your device directly on the page, bringing it to life.

Exclusive Access

These codes give you instant access to videos that will take you beyond the pages of the book to meet the people and experience the places in the stories. You'll also discover bonuses that the text alone doesn't reveal.

No scanner? No problem.

Each QR code has a web address listed under it so you can you can access all these fabulous extras on your desktop or laptop computer. You can go directly to the website www.awakethebook.com and click on the chapters link to view the films.

Introduction Scene One

Scan QR code and place device here or go to zph.com/awake/intro1

Introduction Scene Two

Begin your experience on previous page

CHAPTER ONE

Bring Back the Clowns
September 2006 Haiti

The Woman, Part 1

I watched as they dragged a screaming woman into the dusty streets of Cité Soleil. Stopping directly outside our truck, a group of men threw her to the ground, savagely ripping the shirt from her body. One man jumped in with fists flailing. He was trying to drive away the others, but there were too many. He took a fist to the face, immediately going to the ground. At least ten men were involved in the fighting, but the crowd that had gathered to watch easily numbered more than fifty, and it was growing by the second. My eyes were glued on the woman who was at the center of it all, being pulled back and forth like a rag doll.

Father Rick Frechette—whom I simply call "the priest"—was talking on his cell phone, not yet aware of the brutality happening just outside his eyeshot. Only when a man was shoved against the side of the truck did his attention shift. We were inside a medical truck, and the woman was being attacked just a few feet from my door. Unable to make myself move (and unsure what I would do if I could), I sat and watched as the violence began to spread. Some of the spectators—men and women—were beginning to join in the fight.

The woman was screaming, agony obvious in her eyes as one of the men brought his face close to hers, shouting angrily. Tears mixed with the dust to make muddy tracks down her cheeks. Wrestling an arm free, she slugged one of her assailants hard in the face. Shock shifted to rage as he grabbed hold of her arm once again and slammed his fist into the side of her head. Stunned, her legs momentarily gave way as she slumped between the men.

My breath stopped as a knife flashed from somewhere deep in the crowd. The fighting seemed to be spreading to a much larger group. At least twice as many men and women had now joined in the madness. Less than a minute earlier, only ten men had been fighting, but now there were more than thirty men and women who were shoving and screaming at each other wildly. Yet it was this woman who was at the heart of the chaos. All of the violence was centered on her. I didn't know what had caused it, but that didn't matter. Someone was going to die.

Another man rushed forward, trying to free the woman, but he was shoved hard. Stumbling back, he slammed against the side of the truck and fell to his knees. Transfixed on the scene in front of me, I didn't hear the door opening on the other side of the medical truck. I didn't notice the priest exiting the vehicle.

I've been in a fight to protect someone on two occasions, but neither of those experiences came close to preparing me for what was happening now. With the Haitian woman, life and death hung in the balance. I felt both concern for her safety and powerless over the situation. It was the powerlessness that distinguished this occasion from the time almost ten years earlier. When I was nineteen, I don't think I would have gotten much more than a bloody nose.

Take Your Hands Off the Girl

She was screaming, the sound reverberating off the alley walls. Stuart and I ran to the window. We were three stories up, inside a church in the center of Pittsburgh. It was ten o'clock in the evening, and the church was locked for the night. We were trying to pry the window open, but it looked as if it had been rusted shut for the past twenty years.

I was in Pittsburgh with a team of students who were volunteering with the church for a week. We had been spending our days serving in soup kitchens and helping out wherever needed. The pastor had graciously allowed us to sleep at the church so we wouldn't have to spend money on hotel rooms. Although I'd spent a little time with Stuart, we didn't know each other very well. We just happened to be together when we heard the scream.

When the woman screamed for the second time, she sounded like she was struggling with someone. Stuart and I stared at each other for a moment, uncertain about what we should do next. Stuart quickly darted for the stairs as I followed close behind. The stairs led directly to an emergency exit that seemed to be in the right place. Stuart shoved it open and stepped aside, allowing me to run out at full speed.

My feet crunched on newly fallen snow as I slipped on a layer of ice beneath, barely keeping my balance. I was wearing jeans and a T-shirt, and it was well below zero. I turned, frantically searching for the woman and already feeling the intense cold. Standing next to the now-opened door was a man who stood with his hands clasped around the neck and shoulders of a woman. She was pressed against the wall in the back alley of the church. He was wearing a suit and a warm-looking leather jacket. The woman was dressed in an evening gown that shimmered when she moved. She had golden hair and was quite beautiful.

When the man saw me, he took his hands off her throat and grabbed her by the wrist. I looked at Stuart, who was still standing in the open doorway, looking as scared as I felt. We briefly locked eyes just before he turned and ran, the door slamming shut behind him. The door didn't have a handle on the outside. Stuart had locked me out in the alley with the man.

As he turned, I immediately knew I was in trouble. I've always been the "skinny kid." Throughout my childhood I dreamed of being "the wiry kid" who was hard to pin down in a fight, but this was only a dream. There is a difference between skinny and wiry. Skinny means you just have skin over your bones. Wiry means you have tight muscles under that skin. Wiry kids are cool. This man, on the other hand, was neither skinny nor wiry; by the looks of him he'd probably always been "the muscle kid." The muscle kid has a six-pack by the age of five and never loses it.

Both the man and the woman seemed as confused by my presence as I was. He looked at me, waiting.

With a voice that squeaked with fear I stuttered, "Take ..." I had to clear my throat. "Take your hands off the ... girl." I'm sure my tone was more distressed than forceful.

I'm not sure why I chose to speak like a superhero. It probably came from watching too much Batman on TV as a child. The man looked me in the eye,

the edges of his mouth curving in a small smile. Even the lady didn't seem as appreciative as I would have hoped.

"Get out of here," he said. "Leave us alone or you're going to get hurt." His tone was more irritated than angry.

He was right. This "man" was at least twenty-five, and I was only eighteen. I was a kid from the suburbs who had never been in a real fight. This was a guy from the city. Everyone knows that guys from the city know what to do with their fists. I'd seen *Lean on Me*.

"I can't . . ." He turned and gave me an "are you really still here?" look. Taking a step back, I continued. "I can't do that. You need to let her go." This time I sounded more like I was asking a question.

I spent my childhood dreaming about being in this kind of situation. In my dreams I had bigger muscles and a lower voice, and I was never scared. I'd stare into the mirror, furrow my brow, and then point and say, "Let go of the girl," or, "I guess I'm going to have to teach you a lesson," or, "Prepare to meet Mr. Pain!" I'd practice these and many other ridiculous lines with the desperate hope that I might someday have a reason to say them. I still practice these kinds of lines, but now it's usually while I'm driving, which is much more grown-up.

A moment later, I found myself lying flat on my back in the snow. My jaw was throbbing, and I had no idea where I was. I honestly never saw him hit me. I was looking at him, but the whole "fist coming toward my face" thing somehow escaped my notice. After a moment of confusion my eyes focused on the man. He crouched low and grabbed my shirt. I still didn't know what was happening; to this day I'm not sure if he was trying to hit me again or pick me up and tell me to "run along." I started thrashing around, like a snow angel in distress. Just then the emergency door opened again, and this time there were five men standing in it. Stuart had returned with backup, thank God. When my friends saw me, it looked like I was "wrestling" with the man.

Until now, I haven't felt the need to tell the truth of this story. If they wanted to think I was wrestling, who was I to tell them different?

Although this story is slightly embarrassing, it's also something I'm proud of. I stepped outside and stood up for someone who needed help. Even though I lost the "fight," I lived a story that would help define me for years to come. But when I watched the woman being beaten in Haiti, I don't think I could have made myself grab the door handle, let alone get out of the truck.

Death on the Wind

Hours before the woman was attacked, I had arrived at a hospital in Pétion-ville, just south of Port-au-Prince, the capital of Haiti. I was there to do some research for a documentary I was planning to direct. As soon as I walked through the gate to the hospital, the priest spotted me and asked if I would help his staff load the trucks. He told me we were heading into Cité Soleil with much-needed medical supplies.

In 2006, the priest was the only white man who could come and go in Cité Soleil with relative ease. He was well-known as a man who stood up for the poor and the oppressed. Although this was the first of many days I would spend with him, it was immediately clear that he has a deep affection for the Haitian people. He has lived and worked in Haiti since the early 1980s, and his French/Creole comes more naturally to him than his English.

I followed a few young men up a long, dark stairway to grab some supplies from a storage room. They all seemed to be in a hurry to load the trucks and get moving. Later I learned that virtually all of the men who accompanied the priest on these outings owed him their lives. Every one of them had either come out of gangs or from off the streets. The priest had loved them enough to actually step into their worlds and *be* the love that I usually only talk about.

At the top of the stairs was a storage room filled with portable X-ray machines, crates of medical supplies, and long, rectangular boxes. Only when I picked up one of the boxes did I realize what it was. I had never touched a coffin before. This wasn't one of the fancy coffins I'd seen in movies; this was a thin, long box made of cardboard. I carried it down, wondering if we were going to a funeral. After I loaded it into the back of the truck, I went back upstairs with the young men and grabbed another. In the end we loaded eight coffins and a myriad of medical supplies.

As we drove away from the hospital, the priest told me the story behind the coffins.

"When we drive through Cité Soleil, we often find bodies rotting on top of the trash heaps scattered throughout the city," he said very matter-of-factly. "I started bringing coffins with me because I can't imagine what it would be like for kids who have to walk past these bodies every day on their way to school—not to mention the diseases the bodies spread."

"You find bodies just lying on piles of trash?" I couldn't believe it. "How do they get there?"

"On a bad week we'll find seven or eight, but sometimes it's only a couple," he said. "They are people who've either been killed by a gang or have died from malnutrition or some disease. Most households don't have money for a proper burial, so the bodies are thrown on piles of trash. Imagine what it does to a five-year-old child to walk past a rotting body on a daily basis. That child doesn't have a chance of growing up normally. People wonder how some of these gangsters can be so cruel. Just think about that five-year-old and then see if you still wonder. In just a few years, these boys and girls will be young men and women, and unless someone does something, they will be the next gang leaders of Haiti. So we pick up the bodies when we see them, and we bury them. The people appreciate it, and the kids can walk to school without having to experience that kind of thing."

My mind couldn't comprehend this kind of horror. I didn't say anything mainly because I didn't know how to respond. It was then that he said something I will never forget.

"The current life expectancy in Cité Soleil is sixteen. Can you imagine that?" He knew this was pushing my limits of believability. "The gangsters I'm go-ing to introduce you to are mostly in their early twen-ties. They are some of the oldest people in Cité So-leil."

We talked about many things that day. His words carried a wisdom that can only be found in someone who has given everything he has for what he believes. Over the next few days, I watched as he served the poorest of the poor, his every in-teraction giving them a dignity and respect many had likely nev-er received before. The priest doesn't see himself as doing

zph.com/awake/1.1

anything special. He simply does what the Bible commands us all to do: love with action. Although I work in Haiti often, I'm not able to see the priest ev-ery time I go. Since the first time I met him in 2006 I've been able to shadow him on four separate occasions. Each time I'm able to spend a day or two in his presence I feel like I'm in the presence of Jesus. In fact, when I think about Jesus, I often see him with the face of the priest.

The Woman, Part 2

The woman was on her knees now, tears flowing freely as she struggled to rise. Her shirt was lying on the ground, trampled by the madness that raged around her. A thick sheen of dust filled the air, eerily framing the scene.

Another woman who looked to be much older, with the leathery skin and deep wrinkles of someone who hadn't had an easy life, pushed through the crowd, trying desperately to reach the woman on the ground. Her arms were fully extended, but she couldn't get to her. Two men were holding her back as she screamed and pushed against them. They had their backs to me so I couldn't tell if they were trying to keep the old woman safely away from the madness or if they were angry with her for interfering.

The gathered crowd had changed to a mob more quickly than I could have imagined. Everywhere I looked, people were shoving and punching each other wildly. The madness was spilling into the road as some of the mob began to fight in front of the medical vehicle. I was still frozen in my seat.

As the woman rose unsteadily to her feet, I saw another knife rise high in the air, the sun reflecting off the blade like a mirror. This knife was different from the others I'd seen. The others had been shaken violently in order to threaten; this one was raised with the intent to kill.

That's when the miracle happened. I watched it unfold right in front of my eyes. Out of nowhere another hand shot into the air, grabbing the hand with the knife and stopping it before it could plunge the knife into the heart of the woman. The mob quieted in an instant, like waves suddenly calmed. The man with the knife lowered his eyes with an embarrassed, almost apologetic look. That's when I saw him, the priest, standing at the center of it all. He had walked into the heart of the mob and stopped a

Scan QR code and
place device here or go
to zph.com/awake/1.2

Bring Back the Clowns

murder. He is not a tall man, but he definitely stood above the crowd that day. I watched as he took off his jacket and put it around her. He said a few things to her in a language I didn't understand and then led her over to the young men who had followed him out of the truck. These men were trying to look like his bodyguards but ended up looking like mere boys standing next to this real-life hero. The priest must have instructed them to take the woman home because they all surrounded her and guided her away from the crowd. He then said a few more words to the people, putting his hands on their shoulders and calming them.

A minute later, he was back inside the truck. Putting the phone to his ear, he continued with the call he had been on before the whole incident erupted. He hadn't even hung up his cell phone when he stopped the murder. After the call was concluded, he simply continued telling me the story he had been in the middle of before being interrupted by his ringing phone. He made no mention at all of what had just happened.

Father Rick once told me that much of the world is sound asleep and feeling empty. He said that we are sleeping to what life is really about, and only when we step out of our comfort zone will our talents and abilities be drawn out of us.

I'm desperate to live a greater story. I've spent much of my life fantasizing over what I *might* do and daydreaming about who I *hope* to become. Yet often when I find myself in a position to actually do something about it, I continue my dreaming, too afraid, jaded, or cynical to step up to the plate.

I think most of us want to be more than we are now. We want to be kinder, bolder, more passionate, more assertive. And in our dreams we know exactly what to say or do. Yet when we find ourselves face-to-face with an opportunity to act, we run back to the safety of dreaming, too afraid to live fully awake.

Three

I bet when the Old Testament was written, men and women who had access to it couldn't believe their eyes. The Old Testament was the world's first bestseller. In fact, it was a whole conglomeration of bestsellers put into several scrolls. The marketing was sheer genius. Not only was the Old Testament a "book" of bestsellers; it was a book inspired by God himself—at least that was the story around town.

And then one day, hundreds of years after this book hit the shelves, along came these guys who decided to write a sequel. In Hollywood, great films are often ruined by their sequels, but this group had never heard of Hollywood, and understanding the risks or not, they boldly moved forward.

"Let's call it *the Old Testament, Two*," one of them said.

"No," said another excitedly, "let's call it *Return of the Old Testament*."

"Wait," said yet another, "let's call it ... *the New Testament*."

The New Testament, one of them mouthed silently. "That's brilliant!"

And it was. I've heard the New Testament has done quite well over the years.

I grew up thinking that God's story was already written. These two Testaments, the Bible, climaxed with the epic "Jesus moment," and then the ink, quill, and parchments were put away. The story was complete. From that moment on, we were simply meant to learn how to live out what had been taught in the Scriptures.

No wonder so many of us seem to be "sound asleep and feeling empty." We feel that all we can do now is read the Bible as a textbook and try to learn from it the way a historian studies the writings of ancient worlds. If the story has already been told, then we are all late to the party and the clowns have all gone home. And as a result, we think we have no role to play in this two-part epic adventure.

While in Haiti walking with the priest, I began to wonder if God's adventure series was still being written. Maybe, like all great series, this story is a trilogy. If this is true, then just maybe we're all playing roles in the most exciting installment of the entire story. The third act in any story is always the most intense, magical, and beautiful. And as a general rule, the third act is always bigger than the first two.

I think the story is still being written and that it's epic. It's not over yet. The best stories contain tragedy and comedy, true love and adventure, heartache and joy, magic and beauty. All we have to do is take a look at our world to see that all of the pieces to the best story ever told are in place.

The Book of Priest, Part 1

The Bible is packed with stories of men and women who fully experienced life, who were fully awake to the world around them. They made mistakes; they failed and struggled; they experienced extreme loneliness and heartache; their lives were often messy and chaotic. Yet their lives were also filled with miracles, intense beauty, unheard-of wonder, amazing God-experiences. They lived fully awake lives.

I think I have yet to live a story that truly compares with those in the Old or the New Testament. But I believe it is possible to live this way. I know someone whose current-day stories definitely compare. The priest lives his life fully awake. He would be the first to say that some of his days are filled with failure and struggles, and I know firsthand just how messy and chaotic they can be. I've heard his stories of loneliness and heartache. Yet I have seen insane miracles while I was with him, and he has told me stories of amazing beauty. The priest has collected more God-experiences than anyone I've met.

Many of us have been taught that our lives aren't supposed to be messy or chaotic. We've been told that living safe is better than getting it wrong, and if we are a little bored, well, that's OK as long as we don't fail or make any major mistakes. Yet this isn't living; this is sleepwalking. The priest showed me what it means to awaken to my life. He showed me a new way to live.

And someday, when we arrive in heaven and God shows us the New-est Testament, I wouldn't be surprised if the priest gets a whole chapter. He might even get his own book.

zph.com/awake/1.3

CHAPTER TWO

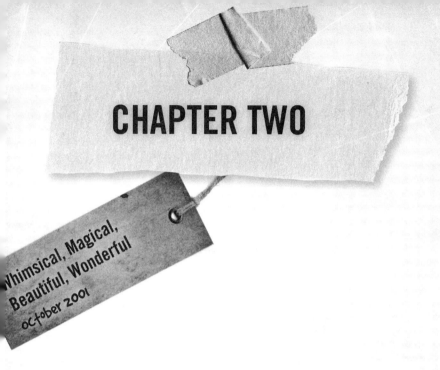

Whimsical, Magical,
Beautiful, Wonderful
october 2001

"Are you awake?"

Even at 2:00 a.m. I could hear the excitement in Douard's voice.

"No, Douard," I said. "Why would I be awake? It's 2:00 a.m."

Wherever he was, it was extremely windy, and I could hear someone yelling in the background. I was lying in my nice warm bed. It was dark except for the soft white glow of my cell phone. There was a pause as Douard waited to answer. In retrospect, I think he meant it to be a dramatic pause, but at that point I still wasn't completely awake, so it went unnoticed.

"Do you remember the last time I called you at 2:00 a.m.?"

My mouth went dry.

"You told me you weren't feeling good. You used the flu as an excuse not to join us."

Immediately my stomach started churning. I reached over and turned on the light, sweat already forming on my hands. I didn't know what to say. My mind began searching for an excuse.

I didn't know anyone who had died recently, so there were no immediate funeral obligations. And aside from my churning stomach I was actually feeling quite good. It was 2:00 a.m., so I couldn't claim to have an "appointment."

Douard wasn't the kind of guy to let me off with a feeble excuse. I'd met him a few years earlier, just a few weeks after he woke up after being unconscious for a few months. He'd been climbing one of the highest mountains in South America when his appendix burst. He was rushed off the mountain in record time and spent the next three months unconscious in a hospital bed. A month after he awoke, he moved to South Africa, where I was living at the time. After getting to know one another over coffee, Douard and I had become close

zph.com/awake/2.1

friends. I enjoyed his company, in part because he was always pushing me to try new things. The problem with this night was that I wasn't sure I wanted to try this "new thing."

The kicker was that I didn't really think he would do it again. The last time Douard had called and asked if I could join him and a few of his friends, I honestly had the flu.

I spent the next few days listening to Douard and the others do that thing—you know, that "man, you missed it" thing. I don't know that I actually regretted not joining in the fun; it was more I regretted not being a part of the conversation afterward. There is nothing worse than sitting around with a bunch of people who have all experienced something amazing or scary or beautiful and having no idea what they're talking about, because "man, you missed it."

"Yes, I'm on my way," I said after a moment's hesitation.

Looking back, I couldn't have said no. Did I want to do it? I really don't know the answer to that. I think that something in me wanted to do it. Would I ever go out of my way to do it? Would I ever be like Douard and spend all that time dreaming it up and getting all the right players together to pull it off? Without a doubt, no.

I've never been an adrenaline junky like Douard. My stunts are usually a little tamer.

The Motto

It was a normal Mississippi summer day, which is to say it was hot and humid and the insects were swarming. I arrived at my job, which basically entailed standing in a trailer with rolls of aluminum and a large bending machine called a "break." I would measure the dimensions of a client's windows and then spend the majority of my day in the back of a long trailer, working the break. I'd bend the aluminum to fit over the sides of the windows and doors. This process is called "cladding," and to this day, I am the fastest cladder who ever worked a break. Yes, I am legend.

I was sitting and eating my lunch on this very normal Thursday afternoon. I had just been telling George about some of my extracurricular activities. George was in his midfifties and was my dad's business partner. He was also my boss.

"I'll tell you what," George said. "I remember being eighteen like it was yesterday. I made some of the best friends I've ever had when I was your age."

"What did you and your friends do for fun?" I asked. I pictured George wearing Depression-era clothes and running in a gang, probably rolling cigarettes or something.

"Oh boy," George said, "I was a lot wilder in those days. The adventures we used to have were just crazy."

I was about to ask him to elaborate on crazy when George said something I will never forget.

"Yes sir, that was the best year of my life!" With that, George got this faraway look in his eyes, and a little smile crept up the edges of his mouth.

I didn't respond. I wasn't sure how to respond. I think George was slightly annoyed with me for not asking to hear some specifics about his glory days.

I drove home that evening in my lime green Mitsubishi Mirage with one phrase repeating in my head: "Yes sir, that was the best year of my life!"

I was eighteen. My year so far, though by no means terrible, was nothing that would ever be talked about at dinner parties. I hadn't really accomplished anything or found something I was terribly passionate about. I felt like I had slept through most of my eighteen years, unable to point to anything worth mentioning. I had kissed a few girls, three actually. I'd kissed three girls — Kim, Celeste, and ... make that two. I had kissed two girls. In retrospect, my slight mullet all the way through high school might have had something to do with that. Still, two girls is two girls.

Up until the age of eighteen I was painfully shy. I moved around a lot as a kid so I never had more than one or two friends at a time. I wasn't even slightly outgoing. My greatest accomplishment was the fact that I had graduated from high school.

"Yes sir, that was the best year of my life!"

"Seriously, is this it?" I thought. "Is this really the most fun I'm ever going to have?" I thought about George. He had a wife and quite a few kids. What about them? In retrospect, I don't think George actually meant that being eighteen was the peak of his existence; I think he was just recalling a good memory and wanted me to drink a toast to time with him. But that's not what I heard.

"Yes sir, that was the best year of my life!"

I went to sleep with those words ringing in my ears.

That night I had a terrible dream. I was fifty years old. I was outside the trailer on my lunch break. I wasn't worried about being fifty and still working on windows. I didn't mind that. In the back of my mind I knew that I had a wonderful wife and a few great kids. But then the nightmare started. In front of me was this dorky, awkward teenager. He sorta had a mullet. I was

MATH CLUB

JOEL CLARK   WILL COURTEN   JESSICA COWL

ELIZABETH BRAND   CINDY BREUL   SAM BRICKFORD

telling him that I used to own a lime green Mitsubishi Mirage. I told him how amazing life was when I was eighteen.

I told him about the time I almost scored the winning goal in my roller hockey semifinal league championship game. I bragged about the time I was promoted from popcorn-popper guy to ticket-tearer guy at the local United Artist movie theater where I worked. I shared with him that eighteen was the year I got an A in algebra. After telling him these amazing things, I leaned back and got this faraway look in my eyes as a small smile crept up the edges of my mouth and ...

I woke up in a cold sweat with one thought pounding through my head: "What if this is as good as it gets?" I don't know if I worded it exactly like that, but Jack Nicholson said it that way, and Jack is cool. And what I thought basically meant the same thing. I just thought it without the help of an Academy Award–winning writer.

I had ambitions and dreams, but they mostly involved working in a career where I could save people and there would be explosions. To be honest, I still want that job, but I now understand that the probability of my getting it is less than 50 percent. I wasn't brilliant in school, and my parents never really pushed college. They weren't against it, but it was never a major topic in our house.

The idea that I was currently living out "my best days" scared the hell out of me. It was that night, sitting in my bed, scared of something I didn't fully understand, that I had a thought that would change everything. It was that night that I came up with my life motto. It was simple, clear, and to the point. I found a journal that I had bought years earlier and never written in. I opened it to the front page and wrote five words—a powerful phrase, the kind you find in movie trailers, spoken by James Earl Jones:

DO IT FOR THE STORY.

The Crane

october 2001

Exactly 2:37 a.m.—I remember looking at the clock and hoping I was too late. I pulled around to the back of the building and up to a closed gate the construction crew had set up to block off the area. I flashed my lights a couple of times and waited. I knew enough not to honk. Douard had warned me not to draw attention. Even though we weren't trespassing or doing anything wrong, it would still be hard to explain to a local policeman what we were doing. After thirty seconds I figured I was too late, and I put the car in reverse.

"This is perfect," I thought. I had the perfect excuse. I could tell Douard that I'd shown up but couldn't get in. Just as I was about to pull away, at exactly 2:38 a.m., the gate opened wide. I drove in feeling a sense of impending doom and wondering if there was a toilet nearby. I'd already visited mine at home multiple times before I left the house, but my stomach was still turning somersaults, and I was having trouble breathing normally.

A guy walked up to my door and shone a flashlight that was attached to his head directly into my eyes. He stood there without saying a word, waiting for me to exit the car. I had no choice now. Someone had seen me.

"Hey bro, my name's Jimmy," the guy said as I got out. "Douard's told me a lot about you."

"Oh yeah?"

"So, you ready to do this thing?" Jimmy asked.

"Are you kidding?" I was trying to sound confident. "It's going to be awesome!"

"You don't look so good. Are you OK?"

"Oh, me? I'm fine, never better actually." I was proud of myself. I said this with a straight face.

"Is that your camera?"

"Yes sir," I replied, holding the camera case a little higher so he could see it more clearly. "I can use it to film what we're doing tonight."

He looked at me with a slightly confused expression. "Yeah," he said, "I guess that's what you do with cameras."

"Yep."

Without another word we turned and walked deeper into the darkness. Later I would learn that Jimmy worked for the construction company that was overseeing the building of this skyscraper. I also later learned that Douard and Jimmy had become friends over the past few months. One day, Douard had drawn a sketch and brought it over to Jimmy to show him what he was thinking. Jimmy immediately hid the sketch from his coworkers, and he and Douard went into the back alley to discuss matters privately.

With Jimmy on board with us, we were given permission to enter the skyrise. We had a senior manager of the site with us at every minute. If the owners of the site happened to wake up at 3:00 a.m., hop in their cars, and come hang out in their shell of a building, only Jimmy would have had any explaining to do. Jimmy wanted to do this thing so badly that he was willing to get in trouble for it. In fact, his name isn't even "Jimmy." I changed his name to protect the not so innocent.

We walked up the dark stairs of the unfinished skyscraper, each new floor rougher than the one before. Shafts of moonlight bounced off the bare plaster walls, and each floor brought with it a growing sense of anticipation mingled with fear. Neither of us spoke again on the walk up, and with every step I berated myself for leaving my cell phone on when I went to bed that night.

Rounding a final corner we entered the thirtieth floor. As I looked around I saw someone else with a flashlight on his head. He was standing at the edge of the building where no walls had yet been built. Below him was a fall into darkness and oblivion. As we came closer, I saw that it was Mark. Mark is one of South Africa's premier rock climbers, and he is more of an acquaintance than a friend. He is one of those guys who is so nice and personable that you feel like you are friends, even if you only see him once a year. I only ever saw Mark in moments like this.

"You made it!" Mark said with a wide grin and extended hand.

"I did," I said. "Wow, we're really up here!"

"You're telling me! Have you been up to the crane yet?" He glanced up.

"Nope, just got here. I'm going to walk around and get some footage from down here, then head up for the really sexy shots later."

If I had left it there, I could have walked away with my head held high. One of my big problems in life is that when I am around people I deem cooler than me, I get really awkward. And in terms of coolness, Mark is definitely high on the totem pole.

"Mark," I called. He turned back expectantly. I didn't really have anything to say. I just enjoyed talking with him and decided to call his name.

"I like the flashlight you have on your head," I said.

I could tell he didn't know how to respond.

"What I mean to say is that it's cool. I haven't seen those before, and I've seen a couple already tonight." I glanced over to Jimmy to point to the one on his head. When I did, I saw that Jimmy had another "man, you're awkward" look in his eyes.

"Thanks, Joel," Mark said. "I'm glad you like it."

"I do," I said.

I took out my camera and ran around getting all the establishing shots I thought I might need. I really didn't know what I was doing back then. I had just started my film company and had only learned how to turn on the camera a few months earlier. But I knew Mark and Jimmy were watching, so every now and again, I'd lift my hands, placing my fingers in the shape of a square, and peek through the center. I wasn't sure what this was supposed to do, but it made me feel good.

After I filmed all the shots, there was nothing to do but continue climbing. The stairs weren't finished past the thirtieth floor, so the only way up the final seven stories was by ladder. I kept the camera on a sling around my neck and shoulder and started the ascent. I was scared. I was only climbing seven stories, but I was already thirty stories up. It might as well have been Everest or K2. Breathing came in jagged gasps, and my heart was pounding out of my chest.

"What am I doing here?" I asked myself over and over again. Not knowing how to respond, I let the question hang.

The crane was still a couple of stories higher than the roof of the building. As I reached the summit of the ladder, I found myself standing at the base of the crane on a small platform. Out at the very end of the crane stood three men on an even smaller platform floating in the middle of the sky. I froze. They were hundreds of feet above the world.

Although the men were too far away to recognize, I knew that Douard, Jimmy, and Alard were the men at the end of the crane. Alard was the only reason I was still considering this insane jump. He is South Africa's best rigger. He spends his days ensuring the safety of stuntmen, builders, and anyone else whose job requires working at extreme heights. Alard and Douard have been friends for years, and every time Douard plans something potentially life threatening, it's Alard's job to ensure that every safety precaution is taken.

Dropping to my knees, I hugged the crane with all my strength, desperately wondering what I was doing there. I turned my back to the men and sat down, trying to regain my bearings. I must have sat there for ten minutes. My eyes were open, but I couldn't see anything. My mind was running frantically while at the same time unable to come up with a coherent thought.

"It's beautiful, isn't it?" Douard said.

I turned around and realized that he had come back to the platform where I was sitting.

"What? Beautiful—oh yes it is, really beautiful." My voice was muffled due to the fact that I was having trouble unclenching my jaw.

Douard smiled broadly. "You doing OK? We're almost ready."

"Dude, I don't know if I can do this," I said, being honest for the first time that night.

"Sure you can. It'll be fun. Do you want to come film over there at the end of the crane? You could get some incredible shots out there."

"Nope," I shot back without a second's hesitation.

"Do you mind if I take the camera and film a little?"

"Be my guest," I said, handing him the camera. I was careful to keep one hand firmly planted on the crane.

While Douard was gone doing what Douard does—being insane for a living—I started to calm down. I could feel my breathing slow down and my heart rate subside. I actually looked out over the city for the first time. I looked out, and I really saw it. Johannesburg at night is one of the most spectacular cities in the world, and I was above it all. The building Douard had picked was the highest in the city. The lights below were amazing. And it was in that moment that I remembered why I was there.

If I had been there to prove something to myself or others, I never would have shown up. If I had been there to get a girl or make a statement, I never would have gone through with it. If I had been there trying to find myself or trying to prove that I had found myself, I would have climbed down to my car and driven home. I was there for one reason, and one reason only. I was there for the story.

The Fall

"Dude, seriously, it's going to be OK!" Douard said this with a look in his eyes that was meant to convey peace.

"I don't want to do it!" I yelled as I literally hung by my fingertips more than thirty-seven stories above Johannesburg.

"You saw all of us jump. Dude, we all made it. It's going to be OK. You're the last to jump. You can do this." Douard was starting to get impatient.

He was right. I had just filmed each of the others on their jumps. Douard had hung upside down from the base of the crane. He had hung like a bat for a moment, and then he let go. Just like that. Jimmy had jumped high in the air as if he wanted to add another meter to his free fall. Alard added an insane amount of slack to his rope and then simply stepped off the crane. I had decided to take my jump style from Mark, who had hung from the base of the crane and simply let go.

With many meters of slack in my rope and another thirty meters of rope attached back to the end of the crane, I hung on for dear life as I pictured those jumps. I didn't want to picture them. I couldn't help it.

"Do you want us to pull you back up?" The excitement was fading from Douard's eyes. By this time I'd been hanging from the crane for a full ten minutes.

"Maybe that's a good idea," I said. "You know?"

That's when Mark arrived back at the top. He had been listening to our conversation.

"Joel, look into my eyes for a minute," Mark said over Douard's shoulder.

I did look, but only because I was tired of looking at Douard, and I definitely didn't want to look down again.

"When in the world will you ever get a chance like this again?" Mark said this with a surety in his voice that was surprisingly quite calming. "This is a story you will talk about for years. You don't have to do it. There's no shame in coming back up, but you know you will regret it if you do."

When Mark said those words, I remembered once again why I was hanging what seemed like miles above the earth with nothing but a thin static line, a free fall, and a "swing" that has more g-force than the takeoff of a Boeing 747. I was there for the story.

Without another thought and with Douard midway through yet another encouraging statement, I did it. I let go. Just like that. And there, at the end of

Scan QR code and place device here or go to zph.com/awake/2.3

Whimsical, Magical, Beautiful, Wonderful

my free fall, swinging wildly above Johannesburg, I whooped and hollered and then sat back in my harness, spread out my hands, and praised God. I wasn't just excited or feeling a surge of adrenaline (though both those things were true); I was feeling more fully awake than I had been in some time. In my jump from the crane, I experienced a taste of both wonder and beauty.

I believe with all my heart that life is meant to be saturated in beauty and wonder. I often tell my friends that if they aren't experiencing magic and whimsy on a regular basis, then they're in need of a change. I'm not implying that we won't experience pain and heartache. These things are real in every story, whether we choose them or not. But I believe the majority of our stories should be painted with the brush of beauty, magic, wonder, and whimsy. I think these four words are some of the bare necessities of a life well lived. Whereas heartache is inevitable, beauty is a practical choice, and it must be cultivated.

The Bare Necessities

- *Beauty* is anything that makes our souls sing. It is that thing that causes us to spontaneously clap our hands or grin in pure delight.

- *Magic* is everything that is beyond our understanding yet awakens a hunger and curiosity deep inside of us.

- *Whimsy* is the brush that paints our days. Whimsy is the playfulness, the imagination, and the humor that cause us to not take ourselves too seriously. Whimsy has the ability to bring light to any dark situation.

- *Wonder* is the ability to have an attitude of awe and fascination. When we keep wonder in our hearts, we are never too old or too experienced to learn something new.

I spent much of my first eighteen years sleeping to the wonder of life. I went through virtually all of my schooling without ever taking a serious risk. I'm not talking about jumping off something; I'm simply talking about living. Playing it safe for eighteen years led to more regrets than any eighteen-year-old has the right to have.

The Sleeping Regrets

7th grade—I wanted to give Vicky Hicks a hug all year long. At the end of the year, when she told me that her father had gotten a new job and she would be moving away, I was desperate to stand up and give her a hug good-bye. But I didn't stand, and I didn't give her a hug. I regret that I was too shy to hug Vicky Hicks.

8th grade—I didn't call Ben Horner for an entire year. I was incredibly lonely and needed a friend, but I wasn't sure I would like Ben. At the end of the year, we were forced to spend time together. Within a few hours, Ben became one of the best friends I had ever had. I regret that I missed out on a year of memories.

9th grade—I regret not jumping off the tree into the reservoir. It was really high. I sat on the branch for a full hour before I finally climbed down.

10th grade—When my family moved from New York to Mississippi, I was forced to leave the first girlfriend I'd ever had. Although we had only dated for a couple of months, I still wasn't sure she liked me enough to date long-distance. I regret that I was too insecure to call Kim and at least talk about it.

11th grade—I regret my seventeenth birthday. I didn't have a single friend to invite from my new school. Although I had been there for almost seven months, I'd been too reserved to make a friend. My parents—feeling sorry for me—invited their friends as well as my older brother's and sister's so that maybe I'd feel like I had friends. But everyone knew the truth.

12th grade—I regret not asking Celeste out to dinner after I took her to the dance in the twelfth grade. Almost fifteen years later, I heard she really enjoyed the dance, but on that night, I was sure she was ready to go home as soon as the dance was over.

Looking back, most of my regrets involve relationships or life experiences I chose to walk away from. And though I definitely have other kinds of regrets as well—times where I chose to do the wrong thing—the ramifications of those actions were obvious. When I chose to sleep to life, I didn't understand that my choices would define me for years to come. Before I started to "do it for the story," my world was pretty drab. I didn't have a lot of purpose or meaning. I asked questions like, "What if this is as good as it gets?" Once I decided to wake up, to embrace the beauty of my story, those questions no longer plagued me. I think that every time we sleep to opportunity, we lose a chance to define ourselves.

I had no idea at the time, but my choice to "do it for the story" would drastically change my life. Where there had been monotony, now there was magic. Where there had been lack of meaning, now there was wonder. I'm not for one second suggesting that we all drop what we're doing and find a crane to jump from—for me the crane was just one more way to embrace my story. But most of my regrets involve walking away from relationships or *carpe diem* moments. I think the key in "doing it for the story" is simply *doing* something—taking the risk, watching for the door that will lead you into a new experience and revelation. For we define ourselves not by who we hope to become but by the stories we choose to live.

Do it for

the story.

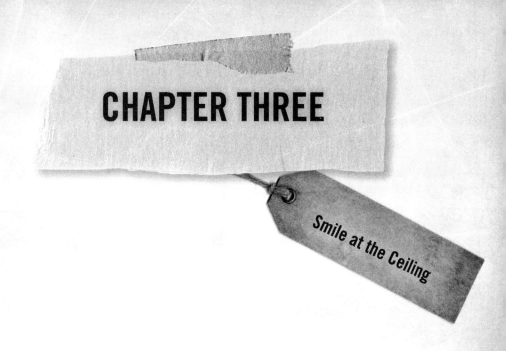

CHAPTER THREE

Smile at the Ceiling

My dad grew up in Canada, that wild country above the 49th parallel. Canada is a wonderful place for many reasons, but what I love most about Canada is its lack of rules. In America we love our freedom, but our particular brand of freedom seems to breed a lot of laws to make everyone feel free all the time. In Canada they just forget about the laws and let everyone figure it out for themselves.

My dad spent his childhood in Ingersoll, Canada, a little town that looks the same today as it did back then. I spent many holidays there, splashing in the creeks and playing in the woods just outside town. I remember running around the quiet streets and imagining my dad as a little boy. I wanted to see the places he talked about in his stories.

My dad spent much of his childhood doing what kids do: getting into trouble. From the stories he told us, I think my dad and his siblings would have been considered wild, even by Canadian standards.

Scan QR code and place device here or go to zph.com/awake/3.1

AWAKE

I remember sitting around the dinner table as a child with my brother and sister, begging my dad to tell another one of the stories from those rowdy days in Ingersoll.

"Tell the story about shooting the kids in the ankles with your BB gun!" my brother, Jason, would beg.

"No," my sister, Aimee, would holler, "tell the story about when you met Mom!"

This was a family favorite. The story of our parents' romance was one that each of us could recite in our sleep. It was in New York City that they first realized their love for each other. It was in the middle of winter with the snow falling softly that they first held hands. It was a love that was truer and deeper than any love had ever been.

"Tell the one about the time you found the man's thumb—the man who tried to jump on the train outside your house!" Jason loved that story. Aimee would scrunch up her face in disgust.

"No, tell the story about running away from the police!" I'd scream.

My mom would smile at us as she dished more stew onto our plates. She'd smile even wider for my dad. I think my dad always knew what story he wanted to tell. He would wait until his audience requested the correct one, until we were perfectly primed, and then he would launch into it.

"We spent almost an hour getting the pile of snow to the edge of the roof of the church," my dad would say, leaning forward slightly, a mischievous look in his eyes.

"It was the biggest snowball yet," Jason would murmur, "bigger than a man."

"Yes, bigger than a man!"

Aimee would lean forward in anticipation as Jason's eyes would go wide as saucers. We knew what was coming, but it didn't matter—the story was perfect every time.

"Your Uncle Bob's job was to stand on the other side of the street and give us the signal."

In my head I could see my uncle dressed in a dark wool coat, fingerless gloves, and maybe even a thug hat. He would walk nonchalantly across the street and stand against an old-fashioned light pole.

"Your Uncle Barney and I crouched real low so we wouldn't be seen high up on that roof. Once the massive snowball was ready, we sat and waited for the choir to finish their final song."

Jason would start rocking in his chair as I grasped Aimee's hand. She'd squeeze it slightly to let me know that everything was going to be OK as the stew in our bowls went cold.

"You didn't see the policeman!" one of us kids would shout.

"He was hiding around the corner. It was our third week at that particular church, so it made sense that the policeman would be waiting. But this one was smart. He was hiding until the perfect moment."

My dad would look out the window as if he could see him even then. I could also see him, my imagination going into overdrive as I pictured the policeman crouched low, watching my dad and his brothers.

"From high up on the roof, we heard the sound of the doors opening. Your Uncle Bob threw his hands high in the air, waving them frantically. He was telling us to wait, but we thought he wanted us to push! With our backs to the giant snowball, we heaved with all our might. It shifted. It groaned. And then we heard it—the crunching of the great ball as it lurched into the air." My dad would stand excitedly, beginning to speak faster. "The families were just leaving the church; it was perfect!"

"BOOM!" Jason, Aimee, and I would yell together.

"BOOM!" my dad would say even louder.

"From the rooftop we saw the policeman dash out from his hiding place and chase your Uncle Bob behind the church. We realized we had to make a break for it, or all would be lost! Without a thought for our safety, your Uncle Barney and I jumped from the roof, landing hard in a pile of snow. Just then, Uncle Bob rounded the corner at a full-out run, the policeman only seconds behind him. As I tried to stand, your uncle plowed right into me, knocking us both to the ground. Looking up, I saw your Uncle Barney look at us and then look at the policeman; without a second thought, he turned and ran, leaving us there."

I could picture my uncle running away, leaving his brothers behind. I wondered if he felt like Judas just after he betrayed Jesus. I wondered if he would ever be able to forgive himself.

"The policeman grabbed us both by our jackets, standing us up."

" 'DON'T LET HIM SEE YOUR FACE, LLOYD!' your uncle screamed at the top of his lungs."

I could picture him there, held up by the scruff of his neck, trying to shield his face so he wouldn't be recognized; yet still calling my dad by his real name. We would laugh until we cried, my dad too, wiping tears from his eyes as he continued the story.

"Your Uncle Bob kicked the policeman hard in the shin, and in a moment of shock, he let go, and we ran!"

This story ends with my dad and his brother in the bushes late at night, hiding from the police flashlights. The moment my dad would finish his story was one of those moments when all seemed right in the world.

A Timid Impression

My dad's stories had all the elements of a great tale—adventure, danger, heroes, villains, twists, and surprises, and usually just the right amount of lawbreaking. Every night at dinnertime he would paint scenes of daring exploits, comedy, and true love. We devoured them all. We knew each one by heart. And night after night I would go to bed with the thought echoing in my head, "What am I going to tell my kids?"

As a child, I didn't get into much trouble. There was no way anyone who knew me would have described me as "daring" or "adventurous." I grew up going to church a lot, but in my dad's stories the church kids got big piles of snow thrown on their heads by the cool kids with the adventures.

Most of my childhood was dogged by feelings of inadequacy, and I was extremely shy. Add to that my recurring thought—"I don't have any stories like Dad's"—and you've got a no-fail recipe for insecurity.

In Full Bloom

In September 1995, just two months after I'd come up with my shiny new motto, I enrolled in a one-year mission training school in Arkansas. I chose to go to the school because I wanted to put my motto to the test. I was desperate to collect some stories of my own, stories that might even compare with my dad's. From what I could tell, this school seemed like the perfect place to get some. It was called Youth With a Mission, YWAM for short.

I arrived at the school with my mullet in full bloom and my insecurities on my sleeve. I hadn't had a real friend for a few years. I hated the way I looked. I had big teeth, a bit of an overbite, a long head—and did I mention the mullet?

On one of my first nights at the school—well past lights-out—a small group of us sneaked out of our dorms so we could hang out in the dining hall. I remember being excited that I was on the "invite list." I wasn't used to hanging with the cool kids who broke curfew. I remember sitting quietly, listening to everyone talk. I could point out the different types of people in the room just by looking at them. This was something I was quite good at in my early years. I could glance around a room and pick out the confident kids in a matter of seconds. I'd watch them and longingly wonder, "How do they always know what to say?"

Off to my right was Kurt, the sporty guy who had great hair. I knew he was sporty because he had a muscle shirt along with the corresponding muscles. Next to Kurt was Noel, the "artsy" girl. She had dyed her hair a deep maroon, and her clothes looked like something from the 60s meets the 90s—very artsy. Over to my left was Amy, the cute girl who obviously knew who she was and wasn't afraid to speak her mind. I knew this because she was speaking her mind in that very moment, sounding very sure of herself. Beside her was Sandy, the cute Latino girl who was sincere and very accepting. She had even gone out of her way to come say hi to me earlier that day. Next to Sandy sat Jeff, the alternative, trendy guy. I'd only met him for five minutes, and already I knew more about underground, alternative Christian music than most underground, alternative Christian musicians probably know. Next to Jeff, and off to my left, were Jason and Tricia, a young married couple who were just plain cool. Jason had enough chest hair to braid and Tricia kept coming up with witty one-liners. And then there was me—the guy who dressed badly and had ridiculous hair, big teeth, and a long head, the guy who didn't know much about anything and was passionate about nothing.

I watched as everyone around me talked with a confidence I had rarely felt in my life. Usually in moments like that I would sit quietly and listen. I'd laugh at the appropriate times and then go to bed and wish I knew at least a little of who I was. On this night, I decided to put my motto to the test. I decided to have a mini-adventure right there in the dining hall. I decided to "do it for the story."

With voice shaking, I jumped right into the middle of the conversation. "I used to have a paper route when I was twelve!" I said a little too enthusiastically.

The group suddenly stopped their chatter as everyone's eyes shifted to me. Sporty Kurt had just been telling Artsy Noel about an overly large spider he had seen in the kitchen.

"One night, my sister, Aimee, decided to show me the movie *Arachnophobia*." I was talking as fast as a man on fire, adrenaline surging through my veins like never before.

"Dude," Alternative Jeff broke in, "that movie scared me when I was a kid!"

"The next morning when I went out to deliver the papers, I walked between two really big trees. Strung between them was a massive spiderweb with a huge spider directly in the middle. And I walked right into it!"

Sincere Sandy's eyes popped as Sure of Herself Amy's hands went to her mouth.

"The web literally covered my head, with the spider sitting on the bridge of my nose!" I was motioning with my hands, trying to remember the way my dad looked when he told a story.

Chest Hair Jason's face went from interest to shock. Even Witty Tricia looked horrified.

"I screamed like a little girl and began slamming my hands into my face. I must have run at least half a block, just screaming and hitting myself."

The entire group burst into laughter. It wasn't feigned, and it wasn't polite; it was the hearty kind of laughter that doesn't end with a "well, that's me; I'm off to bed" type of comment.

zph.com/awake/3.2

It was then that the magic happened.

"Dude, great story," Alternative Jeff said with a grin. "That reminds me of the time I was working with my sister ..." Jeff continued talking, telling another story of an overly large spider. But I didn't hear. Jeff's words were ringing in my ears: *Dude, great story*.

"If only my dad could see me now," I thought.

We talked and laughed for hours before we all went to our beds. The night was pure magic. I went back to my top bunk and lay down, staring at the ceiling with a massive grin resting on my face. I felt something I couldn't explain. It took me a few years to understand what it was that I was feeling, but I knew things would never be the same again.

The next day, something even more magical happened. When I got out of bed and looked in the mirror, I almost didn't recognize myself. In what must have been the first dork-transforming miracle in history, I swear my teeth weren't quite so big and my head didn't seem insanely long. I did notice that my hair was still bad, but suddenly I was motivated to fix it. I went out that very morning and had Noel chop off my mullet. In retrospect, I should have gone to someone who knew what she was doing, but it was really more about the statement in the end.

Everyone has a story like mine. I now understand that even the "confident" kids I used to watch were never as confident as they appeared. Insecurity is a part of growing up. Only when we step out and embrace our stories, when we "do it for the story," can we begin to shed our deep-rooted insecurities. But the night in the dining hall wasn't just magical because my insecurities began to diminish; this was the night when I first felt something that would take me years to define. When I finally realized what it was, it changed everything.

Deepening

I think many people only interact with God in their prayer times or during the preaching and worship sessions at the church they attend. Yet I don't think these were ever meant to be the primary times God interacts with us. In fact, I'm not even sure they are the most important. I think our prayer and worship times are simply meant to be a deepening of what God is doing in our daily lives.

It seems to me that all relationships are built on experience. When I connect with old friends and we stay up long into the night remembering the funny, painful, and downright scary moments we shared, it is clear that our relationships were built on multiple shared *experiences*. I love talking to my wife. She is brilliant and passionate and has more wisdom in her little finger than I have in my entire body. But if all we ever did was talk, if I constantly told her how much I loved her and then she told me how much she loved me, our marriage wouldn't last. Without the physical intimacy, the little jokes, the laughter, the shared dreams—without the lifetime of shared *experiences*—our words would quickly be rendered meaningless.

I don't know many people who would disagree that a major key to a good relationship is shared experience. Yet for some reason, we don't seem to think this is true in our relationship with God. For some reason, we've been taught that the primary way we are supposed to interact with him is through talking, listening, or worshiping (which usually signifies singing). I spent many years approaching God with the thought that our relationship was built only on the "spiritual moments" in my life. As a result, my prayer time, and thus my relationship with God, was disturbingly boring.

My "quiet time" would usually look like this:

Prayer Time for Dummies

1. Read something in the Bible.

2. Tell God you love him. (I often wouldn't "feel" love, but I knew it was the right thing to say.)

3. Ask God's help for addressing those things in your life that aren't going well.

4. Talk to God about "others" who might need his help or might want to get to know him.

5. Always end with telling God how great he is. (This was always a tough one for me. I usually said the same things every day. "God, thanks for creating the world. Thanks for dying for us. Thanks for helping me pass math. Thanks for . . .")

This was the essence of how I related to God for many years. My usual prayers would be quick and slightly awkward, and I rarely felt close to him. The idea of a personal or intimate friendship was just silly. I would sing and talk about God being my friend, but it was in no way true. For many years I was fighting boredom and feelings of guilt about my boredom with God, the Bible, and all things Christian. It wasn't that I didn't believe in him; I did. I just didn't understand how to relate to him.

If relating to God is just talking, praying, meeting with others, singing, and then hearing someone else talk about him, I don't get it. Can this be the entirety of any relationship? I think God is always speaking to us and that if we will listen, we will hear his voice. But I don't just want to hear his voice; I want to experience his pleasure!

I understand that much of our relationship is about faith. I understand that we can't walk around with God's physical hand in ours or go out and have an ice cream sundae and then catch a movie. While he is always there, at least on this side of heaven, my wife snuggles much better than he does. However, if our relationship consists purely of faith in what we're told, what we read, and what we think we hear, without any feeling or experience of wonder, beauty, laughter, magic, or action on our part, then I'm not sure we can use the word *relationship* to define it.

What Pleasure Feels Like, Part 1

If I were to ask you, "What does the pleasure of God *feel* like?" I don't know what your answer would be. But if our only experience with God has been through reading, praying, and singing, then we're missing the most important aspect of our relationship. Although I can't share an ice cream cone with God, I can *experience* his pleasure.

When I was eighteen and staring at the ceiling, a perpetual grin resting on my face, I couldn't describe what I was feeling. I was excited about life for the first time in years, but I couldn't have defined why. It was more than simply having a good time, making friends, and shedding some insecurity. Looking back, I now understand that what I was feeling was God's pleasure toward me. I believe God was sitting in heaven, grinning back at me, as proud as a peacock. I believe that his pleasure amplified my pleasure, and it was in experiencing his pleasure that my life was forever changed.

God's pleasure is addictive. I can't get enough of it. With every dream awakened, I believe his excitement grows. I don't think he's simply excited about my doing something the church has deemed "spiritual"; I think he's excited when I live fully, experiencing the wonder and beauty he has created for me. The four-hundred-meter Olympic champion of 1924, Eric Liddell, understood this truth. In an interview he once stated, "I believe that God made me for a purpose, but he also made me fast. When I run, I feel his pleasure."

The Teacher of Ecclesiastes writes,

```
Seize life! Eat bread with gusto,
Drink wine with a robust heart.
Oh yes—God takes pleasure in your
    pleasure!
Dress festively every morning.
Don't skimp on colors and scarves.
Relish life with the spouse you love
Each and every day of your precarious
    life.
Each day is God's gift. It's all you get
    in exchange
For the hard work of staying alive.
Make the most of each one!
Whatever turns up, grab it and do it. And
    heartily!
This is your last and only chance at it,
For there's neither work to do nor
    thoughts to think
In the company of the dead, where you're
    most certainly headed.
                    Ecclesiastes 9:7–10 MSG
```

God created the world so that we might explore it. He created beauty so that we might enjoy it. He created wonder so that we might experience it. But when we relegate our relationship with him to the times we pray, sing, or read, we miss out on the reasons for our praying, singing, and reading. God's pleasure isn't some shiver that makes its way up my spine; it is a palatable joy found in stepping out and embracing everything he has placed in my path. For when we embrace the story he has placed in front of us, we are embracing God.

I believe that God has placed dreams inside each and every one of our souls. I think that each dream is put there with the express purpose that it be found. The problem is, when we are unwilling to step out in faith, we don't just miss our opportunity to experience God; our dreams stay dormant inside of us.

One of the ways we pursue God is by pursuing the dreams he places in us. I believe that God feels true and deep joy every time my heart is awakened. And when he feels joy over me, I can't help but grin back. A part of the beauty of life is that we never know what experience will awaken one of the dreams hidden deep inside our souls. Every time we unearth a dream, we awaken not only to a deeper and more defined revelation of ourselves but to a deeper and more defined relationship with God. I think it's that simple. Whether we are stepping outside and stopping a knife fight or taking the opportunity to speak up when we would normally stay silent, it may be this very act that reveals a deeper intimacy with our creator and a new revelation of who we are meant to be in this world.

CHAPTER FOUR

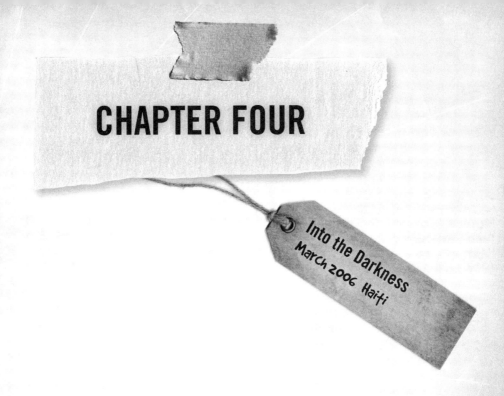

Into the Darkness
March 2006 Haiti

"You may shake his hand," Wisner told me in a voice taut with fear.

Wisner is a good friend. He's also my translator for the work I do in Haiti every year.

"You may shake his hand," he said again. "Joel!" His voice held an edge of desperation.

Although I heard Wisner speaking, his actual words weren't registering. I was too busy staring at the Uzi pointed at my chest. I'd never seen an Uzi in real life, but this one seemed far more impressive than those I'd seen in the movies.

We were completely surrounded by a group of boys between the ages of seven and twenty. Every one of them held some form of weapon that was aimed at either Wisner or me. I remember noticing that some of the guns were so rusty that they probably didn't work anymore, though I definitely wasn't eager to test my theory. As I surveyed the group, I counted four six-shooter handguns, an antique-looking shotgun, and a shiny new Uzi.

"Joel!" Wisner said, placing his hand on my shoulder.

Wisner's touch snapped me back into the moment. Pulling my eyes from the Uzi, I glanced at him, only now realizing that he had been saying something.

"He said you may shake his hand." Wisner's half whisper sounded urgent.

A large man stood in front of me with his hand outstretched and an irritated look in his eyes. I quickly extended my hand, being sure to grasp his as firmly as I could. I didn't want this gangster to think I was weak. He held on tightly and didn't let go. He just looked me in the eyes and waited. Unsure if there was something I was supposed to do, I decided my best option was to meet his eyes and try to look relaxed.

zph.com/awake/4.1

The man's name was Evans. He was much older than the rest, probably close to thirty. He was shirtless, and a large gold medallion hung from his neck. After a moment, Evans let go of my hand and said something with a grin that somehow reminded me of a lion.

"He says you are now the safest person in Haiti," Wisner said with concern still painting his face.

At that, the Uzi left my chest. Apparently, until Evans had given us permission to be there we hadn't been very safe at all. I could tell that Wisner still didn't feel safe, and with all of the guns around us, I couldn't blame him. Wisner had spent the last few years living through the vast number of kidnappings and murders Evans was responsible for. He actually had a friend whose family member had been kidnapped and then killed by Evans and his gang. The fact that he knew what this man was capable of and still agreed to come with me shows just how courageous Wisner is.

Wisner and I had come to Cité Soleil to try to make connections for a documentary my company was hoping to produce. For more than two years, Haiti had been plagued by an astonishing number of kidnappings. Many estimates had the number ranging between eight and ten kidnappings per day. When my business partner and I heard what was happening, we immediately knew we wanted to tell this story.

Unlike Wisner, I hadn't been hearing about Evans and his gang on a daily basis for a number of years. I knew enough to be scared—and even if I hadn't, the guns surely helped—but the whole thing felt more surreal than anything else. Over the years I've learned that I don't react "normally" when I'm in danger. I usually get this bizarre feeling that in some way makes me feel like I'm watching a film. Don't get me wrong, I'm not handling these situations like some pro; it's just that my mind ceases to function properly when I'm in them. When I watch a good film, I'm excited to see what happens next. In this "film" I definitely wanted to see what was going to happen.

Evans walked us through his compound. The place was pretty bare except for a couple of trucks loaded with large boxes. The surrounding walls were painted with bright pastel pictures of Jesus holding AK47s. We were led into a massive shanty structure made entirely of haphazard wooden planks, pieces of tin and metal, and odd bits of cardboard. I had seen many of this type of structure before, but I'd never seen one so large.

As we entered the hideout, I was amazed. This "building" was massive. Just inside the door was a waist-deep, blow-up pool. Sitting in the pool were three pretty women in skimpy bathing suits. Next to the pool was a large-screen TV with a surround sound home theater system. *Black Hawk Down* was playing as we walked in. It was showing one of the bloodiest scenes in the film. It was not very calming.

Beside the pool three men were sitting on crates and deeply engrossed in the film. Only one of them bothered to look up when we walked in. The women didn't seem at all concerned by our presence as they laughed and splashed one another. Evans led us past the pool and through a series of hanging sheets and blankets that divided the interior into multiple "rooms." Some of the rooms had beds, while others contained open space.

zph.com/awake/4.2

As Evans led us deeper in, I remember sincerely hoping that he wasn't walking us to the "special room" where he housed his kidnapped victims. "What an idiot," I thought. "Kidnapping an American has probably never been this easy." I glanced at Wisner, whose fear-filled eyes alerted me that his thoughts were as dark as mine.

In 2006, Evans was, without a doubt, the most well-known and ruthless of all of Haiti's gangsters. The fact that Wisner and I found ourselves not only meeting with the man but meeting him in the middle of his hideout was nothing short of crazy.

Just the day before Wisner and I had marched into Evans's lair I had heard his name when my friend, the priest, mentioned him.

"This guy will shoot you rather than look at you. He's not like the other gang leaders. The others have some sense of decency. I think Evans isn't all there. I think there's something wrong with him."

A few hours later, I was sitting in an interview with a United Nations translator. Apparently, the United Nations troops and Haitian police had been searching for Evans and his men for more than two years.

"If we could just capture Evans, over half of the kidnappings in Haiti would end," the man told me. "The problem is that we can't find him. His hideout is deep inside Cité Soleil."

"Why can't you go into Cité Soleil?" I had asked.

"We send in tanks and armored vehicles on a regular basis, but every time we encounter Evans or his gang, men on both sides die."

"Can't you wait for him to come out of the city and grab him when he does?" I had been trying to think of questions a real reporter might ask.

"Every time we've gotten close to him, he's found some way to escape. After he escapes, he goes crazy. He doesn't just kill people; he finds out who was after him and kills them and then kills everyone they know. The police are too afraid to go anywhere near him. If we could find his hideout, we could capture him there—but we can't find it."

These were the conversations that were running through my mind as Evans led us through his hideout. I don't know if he was tempted to kidnap Wisner or me—or if the thought even crossed his mind—but in the end, he was true to his word. Evans led us out into a small courtyard and had his men bring us two beers apiece.

Sitting in the broiling Haitian sun with a cold beer in my hand, we talked about the potential of doing an interview in the coming days. Since we now had the "opportunity" to talk with the most ruthless gangster in Haiti, it made sense to see if we could actually film an interview with him. We told him we wanted to ask him about the kidnappings and murders that were plaguing Haiti. We made sure to speak about the kidnappings and murders that "others" were doing and to in no way imply that Evans had anything to do with them. The priest had warned us to always speak in broad terms and never say anything that could tie Evans to any of it.

Evans seemed open to the idea, though he wanted to wait a couple of days so that he could prepare some statements he wished to "say to the Haitian people."

Restaveks

When our flight landed in Port-au-Prince over a week earlier, everyone was a little nervous. I had brought a crew of eight very talented filmmakers with me to film a documentary on restaveks, a modern-day version of child slaves. The problem was that none of us had ever filmed a documentary quite like this before. We were in Haiti for one reason: no one else was willing to go.

My client had tried to send four different production teams over the past year, and each had pulled out at the last minute. Haiti has been in some form of tumult ever since Columbus "discovered" it in 1492. The recent upheavals were some of the worst in the past half century. Kidnapping was at an unimaginable high. Gangs ruled the streets, and people were only

Scan QR code and place
device here or go to
zph.com/awake/4.3

leaving their homes when they absolutely had to. The country was literally at a standstill.

My client called me just two days before we hopped on a plane to Port-au-Prince.

"Joel, I think we need to pull the plug on the documentary," she said with an obvious heaviness in her voice.

"What's going on? Did something happen?"

"My contact over there, Jean Marc, just told me he's never seen it this bad in his lifetime. He thinks it's too dangerous for you to go right now. His good friend was just killed in the street right outside his house."

I didn't speak for a moment. I hadn't prayed long and hard about this opportunity, but from the moment it was offered, I felt a strong peace. I also knew that I wanted to shoot it. This was a great opportunity for us to define ourselves as a company.

"If it's all the same with you, I'd still like to shoot it," I said.

Was I being stupid? Maybe, but so far God had blessed much of my seeming stupidity and I knew that the issue of child slavery was on God's heart. I had no doubt that he cared about these kids and wanted someone to tell their stories.

"Joel, I am still open to you going, but you need to know something. We don't have kidnapping insurance for freelance workers." She said this in a very serious and sober voice.

"Kidnapping insurance?" I didn't know that such a thing existed in the first place, so the fact that we wouldn't have it didn't seem like such a loss. "Don't worry about it," I said. "I understand."

There was a definite pause before she responded.

"OK, I guess we're going to go for it."

I hung up the phone and thought of my motto: *do it for the story.* Whatever was going to happen next would carry with it a story that was beyond anything I could imagine. I had no doubt that this was a story I wanted. I called my business partner and then everyone else in the crew. I told them that I was sorry but we couldn't afford kidnapping insurance. I told them that I would understand if they wanted to back out.

All of the crew voiced their disappointment, but in the end they still wanted to go. Our team was set, and we were off to Haiti. We ended up spending ten days driving and flying all over the country. We shot numerous interviews with kids who were slaves and adults who were owners. It was sobering and horrible and amazingly meaningful. We ended up finishing our shoot well ahead of schedule, and we still had five more days in the country.

zph.com/awake/4.4

The Book of Priest, Part 2

Four months before I arrived in Haiti, a friend offered to introduce me to someone she knew who was living there. To be honest, when she told me about the guy, I wasn't sure I believed her. She made him sound like a combination of "Jesus meets Rambo." Apparently this guy was a priest, a doctor, and a hostage negotiator. She told me that he worked in the poorest and most dangerous slums of Haiti. Excited about the opportunity, I promised her I would call him if we finished our shoot early.

To be honest, I pushed hard to finish our shoot. The more I thought about this guy, the more eager I was to meet him. If even half of what my friend told me was true, this priest seemed to be more awake than anyone I'd ever met. The very second I was sure we had completed the restavek documentary, I found his number and dialed.

"Hello," he said. He sounded slightly out of breath and I could hear someone screaming in the background. "Hello!" He shouted this time. The sound of a man biting back screams was louder now.

"Hello," I said, "I'm not sure you remember me, but I sent you an e-mail a while back. We have a mutual friend, she—"

"What do you want?" he said with an obvious irritation in his voice.

"Well, I, uh, I just wanted to see if we could meet. I was told I should meet you if I came to Haiti and I—"

"I can't talk now. A man was kidnapped, and we just got him back. He was shot in the exchange, and I'm busy getting the bullet out."

I heard another scream. I was stunned. Why would this guy answer his phone in the middle of digging out a bullet?

"I'm sorry, I, uh, I didn't mean to interrupt. I can call back later," I said timidly.

The phone went dead. I hung up slowly, still processing what had just happened.

When I called him a little while later, he set a time for us to meet. In our meeting I mentioned that I would love to film a documentary about all the kidnappings that were going on in Haiti. I knew the priest had often worked as a hostage negotiator, and I hoped he might be willing to offer some insight. My thought was that we would film an interview with the priest, put together a research paper, and then go back to the United States and find an investor for the documentary. If we found everything we needed, maybe we could come back to Haiti a few months later.

To my surprise, the priest was more than willing to help. Although he didn't want to be viewed on camera, he offered to let me shadow him for a couple of days and introduce me to three of the top kidnappers in Haiti. He said he thought they would give some "great interviews."

By the end of our conversation, we decided to begin filming the documentary straightaway. We wouldn't normally dive headlong into a massive project without at least some research, but when I was around the priest, I felt like I could do anything. When he offered to help me get the story, I knew I could go my whole life and never get an opportunity like this again.

It was the priest who introduced Wisner and me to Evans the gangster. He had never planned on introducing us. It just kind of happened (I go into detail in the third link in this chapter). After he introduced us, the priest was immediately called away to respond to another emergency. Before he left, he made Evans give his word that we were "under his protection." Then, just like that, both Wisner and I were left alone with Evans and his gang.

The priest first met Evans at one of the priest's roving medical clinics. Evans had needed treatment for an illness and had nowhere else to go. Later the priest would treat some of Evans's men as well. It was because of these things that Evans trusted the priest. It was because of these things that the priest was able to ransom back hostages on a regular basis, sometimes for absolutely no money. And it was also the reason the priest seemed comfortable leaving us with him.

We ended up spending two full days with Evans. We walked the main streets of Cité Soleil, a place the police hadn't been to in almost three years. Every time we passed a pile of trash, I was reminded of the bodies the priest spent his days picking up. I wondered how many of those bodies had been thrown there by Evans and his men. I remember being unnerved multiple times during those two days. There wasn't a single building on the main street of this 100,000-person city that didn't have at least a few bullet holes. Many of the buildings had been completely destroyed by tank fire and grenade shrapnel. At one point, as we were walking down the main street, we spotted a United Nations tank rolling up the other direction. We all ran behind a building—we with our cameras and Evans and his men with their guns—and ducked low as the tank rolled by.

zph.com/awake/4.5

I wondered at the world then. Here I was with literally the most famous criminal in Haiti. I was under his "protection," hiding from the good guys. I wasn't a trained CNN journalist. I had no real experience in these kinds of documentaries. I was in Haiti simply because I don't use the word *no* very often.

I think a large part of awakening to life, of embracing the fullness of our stories, is simply having an attitude of yes. I understand that saying yes to everything is silly, and of course we should say no to those things that are unhealthy or immoral. But when we can learn to make yes our default instead of no, we're bound to experience more beauty, wonder, and magic in our lives.

zph.com/awake/4.6

I know a lot of people whose first response to any risky, uncomfortable, or unknown situation is no. Yet these are often the same people who tell me they are desperate to have more meaning and adventure in their lives. When I listen to these people talk, I'll often offer some ideas as to how they might awaken to the beauty of life. Before I can finish my thoughts, they will usually break in to tell me just why my ideas won't work for them.

And the list goes on. No one likes to be uncomfortable, and sacrifice will always feel like a sacrifice. But I think that when we allow fear to dictate our actions, we lose out on the opportunity to awaken more fully, experience more deeply, and define ourselves more clearly.

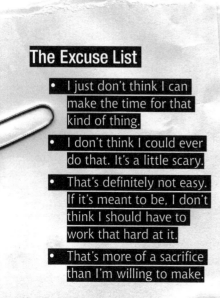

The Excuse List

- I just don't think I can make the time for that kind of thing.
- I don't think I could ever do that. It's a little scary.
- That's definitely not easy. If it's meant to be, I don't think I should have to work that hard at it.
- That's more of a sacrifice than I'm willing to make.

I believe it is experience that shapes us. It is practical experience—doing something—that helps us define who we are meant to be in this world. When we choose to say yes, to awaken to life and embrace the fullness of our stories, it will rarely be comfortable. These choices will always involve sacrificing our ego, time, and energy. Living fully awake lives implies risk, which by its very nature is scary. Yet dreams can only be awakened at a cost.

Nudity in the Lake

The scary movie formula hasn't changed since the invention of the scary movie. It usually opens with some stupid girl who decides to ignore the fact that there is a killer on the loose, and like an idiot, she goes out late at night. She's pretty enough to get your attention, but she's still an idiot. She walks through the creepy, dark forest, takes off some of her clothes, and jumps in the lake. We all know how it ends for her. The other characters in the film then take "idiot" to whole new levels. They spend the next hour and twenty minutes running and hiding and screaming and dying.

I've played each of these characters at some point in my life. I either completely ignored the nagging fear that haunted me and went about living life or I took off my clothes, jumped in the lake, and hoped to be left alone. At other times I chose to do the opposite. I ran away; I hid; I did whatever I could so that whatever it was I was afraid of wouldn't find me.

The problem is that all of these reactions only gave power to that which I feared. I never made myself face my fear and therefore was never able to learn its name. Over the years I've come to understand that what I fear is actually quite simple—its name is "Unknown." And like it is with all scary movies, the second I can put a face and name to the killer, the plot suddenly seems rather silly and blatantly obvious. "Of course!" I think to myself. "It was the janitor the whole time." Suddenly the killer's once-scary mask doesn't scare me at all. The movie's main characters, those who are left, finally stand up for themselves. They stop running and face their fear head-on. And this is where the movie ends. A scary movie is no longer scary when its characters are no longer scared.

I didn't understand it at the time, but the day I decided to "do it for the story" was the day I decided to stop running from or ignoring my fears. When we walk through life afraid, it makes sense that our default answer to virtually any question will be no. But the future is the great unknown. James 4:14 reads, "Why, you do not even know what will happen tomorrow. What is your life? You are a mist that appears for a little while and then vanishes."

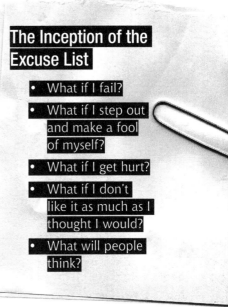

The Inception of the Excuse List

- What if I fail?
- What if I step out and make a fool of myself?
- What if I get hurt?
- What if I don't like it as much as I thought I would?
- What will people think?

We all give ourselves excuses. But at their core, I think most of our excuses stem from a fear of the unknown. The questions behind the excuses are far more telling than the excuses themselves.

And the list goes on. Living fully awake is scary. Choosing comfort and security is always easier than choosing to face the unknown, but the heart that lives awake sees the excuses for what they are—simple fear.

I still find myself naked in a lake more often than I'd like to admit, but I've also had some amazing adventures that have led to mind-boggling stories. I have run toward the darkness, screaming into the wind that I will not back down. And each time, my soul has been awakened; each time, I've found that God has been waiting in the midst of the darkness, calling me to meet him in the place that once held me captive by fear.

When my friend the priest asked if I wanted to not just interview the most ruthless gangsters in Haiti but spend a few days with them, it was obvious that saying yes would kick open the door to somewhere I had never been before. I knew that wherever this story led, the journey would hurl me headlong, deeper into my relationship with God. Knowing this, how could I have said no?

I think it's that simple. When we have willing hearts, when our answer is yes in that space where we would usually say no, suddenly we find meaning in the midst of our story.

I think it's time to dream big dreams. It's time to chase after them and stand in the face of our fears. For this is where God is found. This is where he is calling us to meet him and experience his pleasure.

CHAPTER FIVE

The Great Couch Scare of 1999

Everything changed when I met her. For many years friends would tell me there was no such thing as "the perfect girl." But I knew they were wrong. I had met her, and her name was Megan.

Megan and I first connected at a summer camp when I was eighteen. This happened just a few weeks after I'd come up with my shiny new motto. Before the motto I didn't really meet girls. From the very second I saw Megan, the very first second, my eighteen-year-old heart, mind, and hormones said, "That's her, Joel—the one you're going to marry." The week at camp was magical. We were both volunteer staff and therefore didn't have curfews like the seventeen-year-old children below us. On five separate occasions Megan touched my arm with her finger and drew little circles on it as we talked. Circles. She did it while we talked. That is how much she liked me.

The week ended, and we had to part ways—me to my new address in Mississippi, while Megan would head home to New York. Our good-bye was one of those moments where a sensitive viewer would cry if they saw it in a movie. We were sitting in a parked, empty bus. I didn't kiss her. I wanted to, but I didn't want to ruin that perfect empty-bus moment.

"Where do you think you'll live when you're older?" Megan asked. She was always so international and cool.

"I want to live in Africa," I said. I knew Megan loved Africa. I didn't know where I would live in Africa because I couldn't name all the states over there.

"Me too," she said. "Maybe in Tanzania."

"Oh, I've always loved Tanzania," I said, unsure whether it was a city or state.

Then Megan smiled at me in a way I will never forget. Her smile said, "We will live there together, you and I. We will live in Tanzania and make lots of babies, you and I."

"We should go there together sometime," she said verbally. But I knew what she meant.

And then it was time to go. I had been with this girl for a whole week, and at no time did I find the courage to ask for her number. In those days people didn't do the e-mail thing. When we said good-bye, she gave me a very special hug and then walked away and never looked back. I know this because I watched her walk away and never look back.

I suddenly heard James Earl Jones say, "Do it for the story." Then I could see it clearly written in my journal. "What if she doesn't give you her number? What if she laughs at you?" Questions like these raced through my mind. But before I allowed my fear to make the decision for me, I did something astonishing. I ran after the girl, literally.

"Megan!" I shouted. She was half inside the car, neither sitting nor standing. She stopped and looked at me. Part of me wanted to run the other way, but the rest of me agreed with James Earl Jones.

"Hey," she said.

"Can I get your phone number?" I could see her mom smile inside the car. My cheeks flushed. A definite confused look crossed Megan's face, yet she was considerate enough to quickly replace it with a smile.

"Sure," she said. "Why not? It's 716 . . ."

She gave it to me. I got the girl's number! Apparently Napoleon Dynamite can get the girl in the real world. Or at least he can get the girl's number.

Now in the grand scheme of life, this was quite a small gamble. The worst that could have happened was that maybe she would have said no or laughed at me. But neither of those things happened; instead, a little bit of magic was painted into my life. Just maybe I was the guy who got the girl—the really hot girl. This was a small story to be sure, but who knew where it might lead?

It would be a full two weeks before I would find the courage to call her without hanging up when she answered.

"Hello," Megan said.

"Hey, how are you?" I responded, overly excited.

"I'm great. How are you?" I could tell by her tone that Megan didn't have a clue who I was.

"I bet you don't know who this is, do ya?" I offered.

"No, I don't."

"This is Joel." The silence that followed seemed longer than necessary. "From camp," I said.

Then came another period of silence that actually felt longer than the first.

"Oh, hey, you actually called me," she said.

"I did! So how are you?"

"I'm great," she replied. "How are you?"

Over the next month I called Megan multiple times a week, and we talked long into the night. Sometimes we would even fall asleep while we were on the phone together. From drawing circles on my arm to falling asleep while we were on the phone, such was the journey of our romance. This girl was obviously head over heels in love. Back then, state-to-state phone calls cost ten cents per minute, but I didn't care. Megan was hot and cool and beautiful and international and exotic, and she wanted to talk to me. To me! It was the best ten cents a minute my parents ever spent.

A month later, we would start an actual relationship. I would drive the twenty-hour trip to her house numerous times. Megan was the first girl I ever truly loved. She even kissed me a few times, braces and all. And besides the first few kisses when she actually laughed at me, out loud, I think she might have enjoyed it.

Life was magical and everything was right with the world. Yet I think it was Shakespeare who said, "The course of true love never did run smooth."

And as usual, Shakespeare was right. Exactly one month after we started our relationship, the beautiful Megan suddenly had the realization that she did not love me enough to stay in a relationship. In fact, I'm pretty sure that throughout our entire month, she had never mentioned love at all. And in the blink of an eye, my world was back to one.

For the next few years, my life continued, though at no time was I able to get over her. I spent a year with Youth With a Mission in Arkansas and then went back to Mississippi and took a job as a youth pastor at a local church. I also attended some night classes at a local community college. And while I did go on a few dates over the years, I was never able to move on from the exotic, perfect, just-right-for-me Megan. No one could live up to that girl.

Four Years Later

Four years later, my life was going well. I was still working as a youth pastor at a great church, and I'd had the opportunity to begin collecting stories and awakening my heart to a world of beauty I never knew existed. In short, I was starting to define myself. When I turned twenty-two, I was offered a job in South Africa as a youth pastor for one year. I didn't hesitate. I knew that spending a year in South Africa would awaken my soul to a whole new world of magic.

After I accepted the job, I decided to call Megan before I left. Although I hadn't talked to the girl in over four years, she was still the woman of my dreams. I knew it was silly, but I couldn't get her out of my mind. I wanted to go to South Africa without the thought of her constantly tugging at me. I truly hoped I could talk to her and find out that she was either married or had turned into a horrible person.

"Hello," Megan said.

"Hey, how are you?" I responded, overly excited.

"I'm great. How are you?"

"I bet you don't know who this is, do ya?" I offered.

She was silent for a moment.

"Joel? Is that you?"

This time it was my turn to be silent. I was stunned. It had been more than four years, and Megan still recognized my voice. All thoughts of trying to get over this girl suddenly flew out the window. I was over the moon.

ONCE AGAIN, OUR EVERYTHING SEEMED

Over the following days I would call Megan multiple times, and we would talk long into the night. After a week, I decided to risk yet again and invite the exotic woman down to Mississippi to my sister's wedding. To my complete surprise, she said yes! A week later, Megan flew down and joined me at the wedding as my date.

Once again, our love swelled, and everything seemed right with the world. Though we still didn't live in the same state, one of us would fly out or drive to see the other, and we would kiss and I would dream of our future together. My twenty-three-year-old heart, mind, and hormones knew that this was still the woman I was going to marry.

I never thought of canceling my year in South Africa. I was extremely excited about the opportunity to work there, and I felt like God had called me to go. I was excited about finding him there in the midst of the unknown. When Megan and I talked it through, we decided that our love was strong enough to burn brightly throughout my one-year commitment.

I remember the last time I saw Megan before I flew out to Johannesburg. I was about to board the plane that would take me away from her. Our goodbye hug lasted a full twenty minutes. As we finished our embrace she called me "Lion." It was a fitting name. My hair was curly and wild, and I was very manly. As I walked through the metal detectors I turned and roared at the top of my lungs, scaring all the other passengers. In my mind I thought this would be quite the romantic gesture, something that would no doubt cause every female in the airport to swoon. It didn't play out quite the way I imagined. Megan just smiled and waved good-bye.

LOVE SWELLED, AND RIGHT WITH THE WORLD.

As the plane took off, I had no doubts as to what the future would bring. I would go to South Africa, collect some stories, and date Megan long-distance. Then I would come back home and marry her—the classic hero's journey. This might not have been her plan, but I knew she would agree with me in the end.

Toilets and Running Water

I had decided to accept the job offer in South Africa for two reasons. The first was the obvious one—it was a job offer in South Africa; that's just cool. But the second was probably equally important. While living in Mississippi, I'd started thinking that maybe it was time to move out of my parents' house. I thought that maybe I should get an apartment with a friend and buy a couch.

The thought of buying a couch scared me so much that I would have accepted any job offer that delayed a decision of such great magnitude. For some reason, buying a couch was much more than buying a couch. It was one of those metaphors, one that screamed, "I am done with adventure. Now I will settle down and begin the responsible part of my life. Now I will be a grown-up and sit around in the evenings on a couch." I now understand that there is no correlation between couch ownership and lack of adventure, but this took me many years to grasp.

So I accepted the job in South Africa. I moved to Johannesburg, which is a city in the country of South Africa. It turns out that Africa didn't have a bunch of states after all. It had lots of different countries. And South Africa is not simply the southern part of the country of Africa; it is a country all on its own. When I arrived, I exclaimed to everyone how amazing it was that they had toilets and running water. I think this must be the reason it was so easy for me to make friends.

I taught English literature in a high school and worked as a youth pastor. I wasn't actually an English lit. teacher. I had taken a few night classes at the community college in Mississippi but hadn't learned anything I could apply to teaching yet. Luckily for me, the school that hired me was desperate for teachers, and even such a novice as me would suffice.

One night, my youth group was having a student sleepover at the church. We had planned a late-night, citywide scavenger hunt followed by a sleepover that would be followed by a two-day camping trip in the middle of nowhere. In those days I tended to think more was always better.

In the midst of all this, I was incredibly excited because I had just bought "the ring." I planned on flying back to the United States a few weeks later and proposing to the beautiful, exotic Megan. I was coming to the end of my year, and everything had gone according to plan. Megan and I had exchanged many letters and pictures over the year, and though it hadn't been easy, our love had stayed strong. On the night of the student sleepover, Megan knew I was going to call to plan the dates for my visit. What she didn't know was that one of those dates would include my proposal.

One Hundred Condoms

Just before we started the student scavenger hunt, I called Megan's dad to ask his permission to marry her. He told me he didn't think she would say yes, but I could go ahead and ask. Dads are often silly in this way and don't have a clue what their daughters are thinking. I understood that he was really trying to tell me that he loved me as a son and that I had his full blessing. Besides, I had already bought the ring. This was a done deal.

In South Africa, every now and again, people are hired to stand on the street corners and hand out condoms. They also sell clothes hangers on the

streets of South Africa. I don't question these things; I just go with them. I guess you never know when you'll need a hanger at the last minute.

On the night of the student sleepover, apparently a box of one hundred condoms was thrown into the open window of one of the student vehicles. I don't know much, but I do know that one hundred condoms in the hands of a large youth group can only lead to trouble.

"You may not want to go upstairs," Gareth said with a look of confused delight. Gareth is a good friend, and he was a fellow youth pastor on my team.

"What's going on?" I asked.

"I don't know that I can explain it," he said, "but I don't think it'll go over well with the parents."

I walked up the three levels of stairs thinking the whole time about my scheduled call with Megan. I couldn't wait. As I walked into the youth room, I don't know that anything could have prepared me for what I saw. At first it looked like all the kids were playing with an insane number of balloons. Then I noticed others running around with weird masks over their faces. It was chaos. On closer inspection, I could see that these balloons were, in fact, condoms. Many of the students had stretched the condoms over their faces, while others were keeping forty or fifty inflated condoms floating in the air.

"How do I deal with this?" was my first thought. I knew that one of the senior pastors and a few of the parents were going to be stopping by at any minute, and I didn't think they would enjoy the show. Yet at the same time, I knew I couldn't get upset because this was truly funny. I decided to walk around and laugh with the students for a few minutes. I figured that if I played along for a short while, I could then proceed to tell them to stop and I wouldn't look like such an adult.

I made a few jokes as I walked around and bounced several condoms in the air. I smiled at a few boys who were busy popping them and laughed at the funny masks they had made. I was just about to shift gears and start the cleanup effort when I turned to see one of the senior pastors and a group of parents enter the room. I don't think it helped that I was busy "spiking" a condom on the head of one of the fifteen-year-old girls when they walked in. In the end, it turned out there couldn't have been a nicer, more understanding group of pastors and parents to enter the melee of students and floating condoms. After a horrified look from the entire group, I sheepishly walked over and tried to explain the situation. Before I could speak more than ten words, the pastor stopped me.

"You know what, I don't want to know. I do, however, trust that you will be stopping this 'game' sometime in the near future."

"Yes, sir," I said, "I was just about to stop it now."

With a mixture of confusion and amusement painting their faces, they walked out.

I remember this night clearly for a few reasons. The condoms definitely helped, but what came next is something I will *never* forget. About twenty minutes later, I went to the church office to call Megan, the only girl I had ever loved, the girl I was planning to marry. This girl was about to be on the other side of the phone. It rang six times before she picked up.

"Hello," she said in the sexiest voice God has ever given a woman.

"Hey, baby!" I said. I was still trying to figure out a pet name for her, and "baby" was the best I could come up with. "We just had the funniest thing happen at youth group," I said with a laugh.

"Oh, really? What happened?" she said in a quiet and cheerless voice.

I knew immediately that something was wrong. I just had no idea that she was about to break up with me. Even after I hung up I wasn't exactly sure what had happened. I remember sitting on the office floor with the lights turned off. I sat there and cried.

I still had to take the students on a camping trip after the sleepover. I don't remember much of it except that it was the longest and hardest camp I ever ran. We popped a tire on the way out. We got lost and

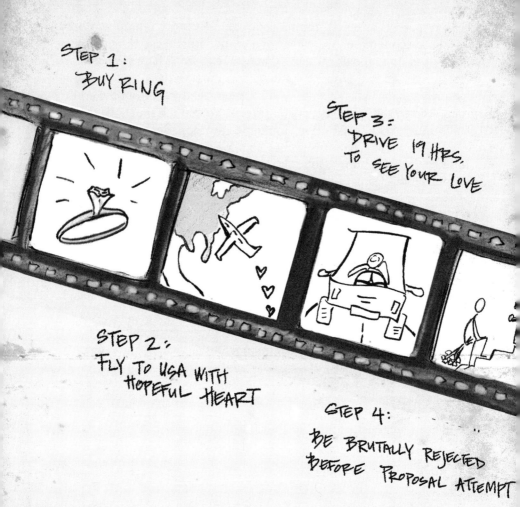

STEP 1:
BUY RING

STEP 3:
DRIVE 19 HRS.
TO SEE YOUR LOVE

STEP 2:
FLY TO USA WITH
HOPEFUL HEART

STEP 4:
BE BRUTALLY REJECTED
BEFORE PROPOSAL ATTEMPT

STEP 5:
MAKE FEEBLE EXCUSE
ABOUT BEING IN TOWN
TO SEE GRANDMOTHER

STEP 7:
REPEAT 2ND HALF
OF STEP 6 FOR NEXT
2 YEARS.

zph.com/awake/5.1

STEP 6:
FIND CHEAP MOTEL
PILLOW TO CRY INTO

had to sleep on the side of the road. We took a one-hour hike that ended up taking us seven hours because, once again, I got completely lost. When we finally arrived back at the campsite, it was well past midnight and totally dark. My mind was numb, and my heart was broken. Once again, the great Shakespeare came to mind: "For where thou art, there is the world itself ... and where though art not, desolation."

It would take another month of embarrassing phone calls and a trip to New York before I fully understood that Megan and I would never make babies in Tanzania and live exotically cool lives ever after. I eventually showed up at her house, thinking that seeing me would somehow change her mind. It didn't. I was in New York at her front door after a nineteen-hour drive. I was there assuming I would have a place to stay. I wasn't invited. I drove away in my lime green Mitsubishi Mirage feeling like the world's biggest loser. I had lost the perfect girl.

Those were some of the darkest days I had experienced in my almost twenty-four years of life. I was devastated. It would take me two more years before I could finally throw away her pictures. That was a season in my life when a cool motto like "do it for the story" meant absolutely nothing. I had done it all for Megan, and she was gone.

I stayed in South Africa working as an English literature teacher and a youth pastor because I didn't know what else to do. My entire future had gone up in smoke. I knew I didn't want to go back to the United States. If I moved there, I would have tons of explaining to do, and I might have to buy a couch.

Over the next few years I would kiss a couple more girls, not because I was in love, but because kissing was fun, and I hoped that maybe it would help me fall in love. Every time I kissed a girl I would call my brother. At least once every eighteen months we would have the same conversation.

"So do you like her?" Jason would ask with brotherly excitement.

"Yeah, she's great—I guess," I would respond without much enthusiasm.

"Have you kissed her yet?"

"Yep, I like the kissing part of being with her."

"Yeah, I've always been a big fan of the kissing part myself," he would say. "Do you think this is going to get serious? Do you like her enough to *really* date her?"

"No, I don't think so. She's great. I just don't like her enough, you know?"

Jason would stay silent at this point. He knew what was coming.

"She just doesn't hold a candle to Megan, you know?" Each time I said this I would feel like the world's biggest idiot, actually I think the word is *chump*. How many years had I spent loving this woman who had broken my heart twice and who had more than likely never thought of me again?

"Yeah," Jason would sigh. "I promise that you'll meet a girl who will measure up, and when you do, you'll forget all about Megan. But there's no rush, you know? You will meet her when you meet her."

Jason is the world's greatest older brother. He never bad-mouthed Megan and never made fun of me for not getting over her. He simply let me grieve in my pathetic way and encouraged me through the process.

The Great Racquetball Player

In South Africa I had a few friends who loved to play racquetball. I was never any good at it, but every once in a while when they needed an extra person, I would get a call. The game happens inside a small room with a high ceiling. The idea is that you are supposed to hit the ball—hard—and it will ricochet off one or more surfaces. The ball changes direction continuously.

A few weeks after Megan had broken up with me for the second time, I found myself in the middle of a game. I was miserable. I remember slamming the ball as hard as I could, taking my anger with Megan and transferring it onto that little blue ball.

I remember feeling like I was that ball. I felt like I had run full speed toward something I desperately wanted, and then out of nowhere I slammed into a wall I never saw coming. I had boldly chased the dream in my heart. I had put my motto to the test, and it had failed me.

I believe everyone feels this at some point. We pursue that thing that awakens our heart—a job, a relationship, or something else entirely—but then something goes terribly wrong, and we slam into a wall we never saw coming. These are dangerous moments for an awakened heart. We have thoughts like, "Perhaps if I hadn't risked so much, things would have been better," or, "Maybe if I hadn't been so bold, I wouldn't feel like such a loser now." And in these moments we will be tempted to fall back to sleep and once again begin dreaming our way through life. These are the moments when the fear and insecurity we overcame to pursue the dream raise their ugly heads and shout, "I told you so!"

When I was eighteen I made the choice to "do it for the story," and though this choice has slammed me into more walls than I can count, it has also given me amazing experiences that have awakened my heart to a deeper relationship with God. It's probably possible to walk through life and never boldly pursue dreams. It's probably possible to completely sleep through life, but I've begun to learn that even the walls aren't all bad. Years later, I look back on many of my dreams that never materialized and see them with new eyes. With the perspective of time, I can begin to see a greater picture of what God might have been doing.

I find it hard to change the direction of my life once I'm headed somewhere. Even if I don't like where I'm going, it's often easier to continue than to stop and evaluate, and it is always easier to continue than to change direction. Yet when God closes a door, when we hit a wall, the only options available to us are to either pursue a new dream or to give up on risk altogether. When Megan broke up with me, I now believe it was God's grace. If she hadn't broken my heart, I would never have stopped to reevaluate my life. And if I am being honest, my life really needed some evaluation. The only "value" I had was Megan. I didn't know who I was or what I wanted apart from her. I was living for Megan and hoping the rest would work itself out.

With many of the walls I've hit, I've ricocheted out into a new direction. Each time I've done this, it's been painful and disorienting. But I've begun to wonder if I ever would have found my new direction if I hadn't hit the wall so hard. I think God has used my enthusiasm to open myself up to every opportunity. Maybe he has allowed me to hit the wall—hard—so that he can more easily guide me into something new, something so much greater than I could ever have imagined. Maybe the death of some of my dreams was a good thing.

five minutes
in this water
will cause
hypothermia;
ten minutes
will kill you.

CHAPTER SIX

Sloppy, Haphazard, Wonderful
November 2007

The sea was rolling, the waves easily topping twenty feet. Keeping our footing on deck was an art that none of us had yet come close to mastering. Staying as low as we could, we took slow, careful steps forward. Waves broke over the side, slamming into us, threatening to sweep us overboard. Falling into this water would have been sure death, even without the storm. We had just spent the last twenty-four hours navigating between some of the world's largest icebergs, some as large as ten miles long and more than one hundred fifty feet high.

The captain's words rang in my mind as we wandered out to the bow. "Five minutes in this water will cause hypothermia; ten minutes will kill you," he had said gruffly. "If you fall overboard, it will take a full twenty minutes to turn this ship around. Don't fall overboard." With that he walked away. All that was missing was the eye patch, and he would have been the perfect captain.

Scan QR codes and place device here or go to zph.com/awake/6.1 and zph.com/awake/6.2

It was warm inside the main cabin, and though I felt the continuous need to vomit, there was no imminent threat of death. Outside, the winds whipped the sea into a frenzy. Every thirty seconds or so, a thunderous, deep clanging would shake the boat as the massive propeller blade lifted fully out of the water.

Rounding the starboard side, we held tightly to the rail as the boat surged sideways. None of us wanted to miss the chance to get storm footage. I stopped for a moment, truly seeing what was happening. My crew—the team I had put together to come to this place—was holding tightly to the bow, completely soaked. We were on our way to Antarctica, the setting for a sitcom we were going to film.

"This is insane!" Kasey's grin split his face in two. Kasey is a great friend and one of the best cameramen I've ever seen. He had joined me on this trip to both film and cowrite the series.

"What are we doing here?" Bryan yelled as the propeller clanged, sending a thunderous shudder throughout the entire ship. Bryan was "the talent," the funniest human currently alive as well as the best actor I know.

Kasey slowly made his way to the side rail as I edged over to the middle of the bow and locked one foot into the anchor housing—this would keep me steady while I worked the camera. We needed to get our shots of Bryan as quickly as possible. The cold was intense, and the wet deck definitely didn't help. Just as Bryan opened his mouth, a massive wave broke over us, once again soaking everything.

This wasn't the first series I had directed. Just four years earlier, I found myself directing a series in South Africa. The difference was that this time I actually knew something about filmmaking.

Ridiculous Works

I moved to South Africa because I was afraid to buy a couch. I had no idea that it would soon become the place I would most naturally call home. While there, I worked as a youth pastor known for being edgy. I really liked this new label, and I did everything I could to make sure it stuck. Among my edgy moves were conducting an eight-week series on the film *Fight Club*, taking more than one hundred students skydiving, leading countless camping and mountain-climbing trips, and convincing the senior pastor to let me build a climbing wall on the outside of our three-story church. In short, I began to learn a little about who I was and what I was capable of achieving.

I had only planned to live in Jo'burg for a year, but when Megan broke up with me, I committed to another. That year led to another and then another, totaling almost nine years. I now consider myself as much South African as I do Canadian or American. Every Christmas I scraped up enough money to come back and see my family in the United States, where I would work for my dad to pay off the bills I had accrued over the year. Once again I'd hop in the back of the trailer and go to work cladding windows. I don't know if I mentioned it before, but I am a brilliant cladder.

While in the U.S., I would spend a considerable amount of time answering questions. Everyone seemed to be very concerned about my future: "Aren't you worried about what will happen when your youth pastor gig ends?" "Don't you want to finish your college degree before you're too old?" "Don't you want to get married and be able to provide for your family?" These and many more well-intentioned questions were thrown my way.

My resistance was twofold. I loved the life I was building in South Africa and was pretty sure that God was pleased with my decision to stay. It felt like he was blessing much of what I was doing, and I felt his pleasure in a way I had never felt before. It seemed like what my stateside family and friends called "irresponsible" was actually the most responsible thing I had done in a long while. I remember telling my youth group numerous times, "Because God created you, he knows what will inspire you in life more than you could ever know. If you give your dreams and your future to God, if you do the best you can with what is in front of you—even if you happen to make a wrong decision every now and then—God will lead you into a life that is far greater than what you could ever imagine." I made remarks like this in the "do it for the story" spirit in part because I believed them and in part because I desperately hoped they were true.

And then, one very normal day, I was sitting with Gareth, sharing yet another crazy idea I had for a youth program. As a youth worker I didn't always connect well with churched kids. The church paid my salary, but I tended to gravitate to the rebels and at-risk students in the high schools. It was these students I was thinking about when I came up with my new idea.

"Dude, I'm telling you, we really can do this!" Gareth said. He was always overly encouraging and never let limits faze him. Gareth's default answer to any question was always yes.

"But do you really think we can get a helicopter?" I said. By this point I had learned I was a natural salesman, but this was pushing it.

"If you want a helicopter, get a helicopter," Gareth said matter-of-factly.

"Richard just bought a brand-new video camera. Do you think he'll let us borrow it?" I asked. Richard was the father of one of my students, and he was a filmmaker.

"He loves you," Gareth said. "He'll let you borrow it if you ask."

"But then we still have to get horses, gallons of paint, a bridge, a jail cell, a limo, some food, and—" I was suddenly frustrated. "Dude, it's a ridiculous idea."

The idea was simple enough; it was pulling it off that seemed impossible. I wanted to create my very own reality TV show. I wanted to take students on an extreme adventure that would awaken their souls and thus awaken their hearts to the message of Jesus. The task was beyond crazy. It had just been an idea, but in the end, Gareth talked me into it.

After a little searching, we connected with a friend who offered us the keys to his editing studio and told us we could use it for free as long as we worked nights and weekends. We had never edited before. We didn't know the first thing about it. Over the next month we would log over seventy hours in the studio, holding the instruction book in one hand and the keyboard in the other. In the end, we created our very first film.

zph.com/awake/6.3

We went to seven different high schools and showed the film. At this point I had been working as a youth pastor and volunteering at multiple schools for a few years, so we had access to many of the schools in Johannesburg. From where I sit today, the film wasn't particularly good, but back then we thought it was amazing. The film was meant to be an attention-getter for this new idea—my very own reality TV show. We didn't own any gear, and we definitely didn't know what we were doing. When it came to cameras, lighting, sound, editing, and selling a show, we didn't have anyone on the team with an ounce of experience. But why should we let that stop us? We had the desire, and I had a great motto. Something this crazy must lead to a great story—and it did.

In those seven high school assemblies, to our amazement, almost twelve hundred students filled out application forms over a two-week period. They were desperate to be part of our brand-new pilot series. We decided to call it *Switchvert*. The name didn't mean anything; we just thought it sounded cool.

We ended up picking fourteen of the most outgoing and at-risk students we could find. The final selection process was via on-camera interviews because that's what reality TV shows did. We knew this because we had watched reality TV shows. In the interviews we evaluated their personalities and tried to find a wide range of students, including those who came from tough backgrounds or broken families.

zph.com/awake/6.4

Prison, a Magical Place

For six straight days and nights we gave these students the experience of a lifetime. For example, on day one we picked them up in a helicopter that had been donated to our show for a few hours. We flew them to an empty field, where they were blindfolded and tied together. We then talked them through an obstacle course. While on the course, my team poured over their heads twenty gallons of every bright color of paint imaginable. Near the end of the night, we sat them down and had a group discussion and heard a speech from a motivational speaker.

The days that followed involved paintballing, riding galloping horses across the plains of South Africa, rock climbing, spelunking, orienteering, and even enjoying a beautiful night out in tuxedos and evening gowns. Each day ended with a group discussion and a speech from a different motivational speaker. We filmed the students constantly, capturing their hopes, fears, and dreams.

On the fourth night of our show, the kids experienced something they will never forget. From this point in the story I am going to help you see the experience through their eyes. The entire night was intense, but for the students, it was both deeply impacting and highly traumatic.

The night started off beautifully. The students, clad in their tuxedos and evening gowns, were picked up by a limousine and escorted to a beautiful restaurant, where they were treated to an amazing four-course meal. After the meal, we hopped in cars and headed to a mountaintop location that had been set up to host our discussion time. We wanted to sit under the open sky, with all the stars of Africa shining down on us. We left the restaurant a little behind schedule, and we were in a hurry to meet our speaker. On the way there, our entire convoy was pulled over by the police.

For some reason, these particular police officers on this particular night weren't particularly happy. It might have had something to do with the fact that I was a little rude in my response to being pulled over. I desperately wanted to get to our discussion, and they were taking their sweet time in questioning us. One thing led to another, and they instructed us to exit the cars as they began to conduct a thorough search. I told the cameraman to keep filming so that we could get the students' reactions. The police were upset to find themselves on camera, which I thought was quite funny.

Things were about to go from bad to worse. One of the policemen found a massive stash of drugs under my driver's seat, which was strange, considering the fact that I don't do drugs. I was furious. I remember saying quite a few things that I definitely shouldn't have. I accused the police of planting the drugs in my car, which, of course, they had. During this whole "discussion," my fellow leaders were trying to calm me down—not very effectively.

Before I knew what had happened, all fourteen teenage students, six film crew, and I were led off to a Johannesburg jail cell. The police took our shoelaces and belts so we wouldn't commit suicide. Then they took our fingerprints and gave us blankets to sleep on. I knew we were supposed to get a phone call—I had seen it in the movies—but they took away our cell phones and never offered us a phone. Maybe these police officers never watched movies. One by one, the students burst into tears.

The police had taken our phones, but somehow they had missed one of the cameras. Seeing this as an opportunity for "great television," I decided that the show must go on. Inside the cell, with over half the students still in tears, we sat down to have our final group discussion. We began to ask the students personal questions about their lives. The discussion was simply amazing. These students began to share with more honesty than I would have ever imagined.

And then things went from worse to weird. In the distance we heard someone scream. Our discussion dissolved. The students looked to us for comfort, but I don't think any of us were giving it. The screaming began to grow louder. As it came closer, we could hear the shuffle of many feet accompanied by a muffled groaning and yelling. It sounded like the biggest brawl in the world was directly outside our cell. One by one we began to rise, our eyes moving with the sound of the screams. Those screams were becoming discernible now—full-on swearing and cursing. Above it all was the sound of the first scream we had heard. It was filled with a rage that reverberated along the walls of our cell. The students bunched together in fear. These very same students who had portrayed such a hard-core image were suddenly speechless.

As quickly as it had begun, the screaming stopped. We could hear what sounded like a herd of horses breathing heavily just outside the wall of our cell. Then we heard the sound of a key turning, and suddenly the outer door to the cell banged open. A large, unshaven man was thrown against the prison bars. His eyes were rolled back so that only the whites were visible. I think the word to describe this man was *fury*. Four separate policemen held the man against the bars, yet somehow he still managed to turn and elbow one of them in the chest. The policeman went to the ground, winded. Another officer slammed his club hard into the man's side. The man's knees buckled as the air left his lungs. For just a moment, no one moved.

When I saw the officer fumbling his key into the door, I started screaming at the police, adding my voice to the ever-increasing chaos. When he opened the door wide, the mass of students and leaders immediately shifted to the back of the cell. It was then that the large gangster was thrown inside, the door slamming shut behind him. The three remaining officers who were still standing helped pick up the policeman who had been knocked to the ground and carried him out, slamming the door to the outer cell behind them.

None of us moved as the man struggled to his feet. I'm pretty sure no one even breathed when he grabbed the bars and roared. Every student was as white as a sheet. And for the first time since we had started this program, someone mentioned God.

"Can we pray?"

I don't know who said it. It came out in a squeak. It came from one of the students behind me.

I smiled. I waited a few more seconds, just long enough for the man to turn around and stare daggers at the students. And then I spoke in a slow, sure voice. "I would like to welcome your motivational speaker for the evening; his name is Franco Siani."

It took a moment for my words to sink in. It took a lot longer to calm the students so Franco could give his "motivational speech" for the night. The entire night had been an elaborate setup, and it had worked perfectly.

Franco spent almost an hour telling his story. He had grown up in a rough part of the city and had joined a gang at a young age. His story is intense, absolutely riveting to listen to—especially while sitting in a jail cell. When Franco was in his teens, one of his friends was shot and killed. This incident sent him into a tailspin that ended with him on his knees at the feet of Jesus.

Franco presented the story of how Jesus broke into his life. He didn't preach at the students, and he wasn't at all pushy. He allowed his story to be his witness. All of us left the jail that night with a deeper revelation of the love and power of Jesus. Later, when we talked with the students, many of them said they felt as though God had been speaking directly to them when Franco shared.

Two more amazing days were still left in this particular adventure we called *Switchvert*. The dream that became an idea that became a reality show also became a beautiful window that opened up to a new direction in my life. Behind the edgy risks we took and the connection with the local church and even the impact on the students' lives, there was this joy, this pleasure I felt — mine and God's. I learned that I was absolutely and unequivocally in love with filmmaking. A couple of months later, I would start my company. I called it Switchvert.

What still amazes me is that everything I had been teaching my students was actually true. God knew what would inspire me and fulfill me more than I could have ever known. I never would have dreamed of becoming a film-maker. But when I gave my dreams to him, when I did the best I could with what was in front of me — even though I definitely messed up from time to time — God showed me something that was far greater than I could have ever imagined.

I didn't plot out my life in a traditional way. I didn't go to college and get a degree and then "start my life." I am not against that, of course — my wife has her Master's degree, and she has had more adventures than I could ever hope for. But my story hasn't been written like that. At no point in my first twenty-five years of life did I have the thought that filmmaking might be something I'd like to do. While I was working with students, I thought that maybe I would be a youth pastor for the rest of my life. I found meaning in it. I enjoyed it. But then, in the midst of doing my best as a youth pastor, God opened the door to film.

Baby Steps

I don't subscribe to the belief that purpose is something that must be worked toward. I think if we're expecting that "someday" we will finally be walking in our purpose, we'll spend our lives sorely disappointed. I believe purpose is something that must be lived today. As long as we are doing the best with what we have, here and now, we are currently living out our purpose on this earth.

What excites me about this perspective is that it implies that our purpose is always growing, always expanding. When I first started "doing it for the story," my "doing it" looked like speaking up in a dining hall or asking for a girl's number. But what's been amazing is that with every dream awakened, God has increased the size of my dreams. Just a few years ago, even my wildest dreams didn't incorporate some of the things I'm experiencing now. And when we see life in this way, it changes the way we walk through our days. What we might normally see as a string of meaningless days or weeks is instead an opportunity to awaken more fully to our story, each day building off the day before.

In the words of famed psychologist Dr. Leo Marvin, defining the approach he calls "baby steps," "It means setting small, reasonable goals for yourself. One day at a time, one tiny step at a time." I think pursuing our dreams means taking small steps every day or at the very least every week toward those things that awaken our hearts. If you want to learn a language or write a book or get in shape, no matter the dream, it will only happen when you take practical steps toward it. It will feel slow and will be hard, but this is what it means to pursue a dream.

In my case, I wanted to create a TV show that would give students an experience of beauty, magic, and wonder. I wanted their hearts to open up to the idea that a good and loving God is the reason for this beauty, magic, and wonder. I had spent a lot of time trying to find creative ways for students to experience God in the past. Yet it was in the midst of living out this particular

event that God awakened a dream he had hidden in my soul. And when it was awakened, he once again grinned down at me, and once again I felt his pleasure.

Beautiful Random

November 2007

Yet another Antarctic wave came crashing down, momentarily baptizing us with its icy spray. The boat heaved and seemed to skitter, at one moment gliding smoothly down the crest of a wave, only to collide with another, each collision sending yet another wave shattering into a million pieces.

"This is amazing!" I screamed over the wind, unsure whether I was more afraid or awed. We had just shot a brilliant, hilarious segment with our main actor, Bryan.

Both Kasey and Bryan were laughing now. The magic of this place was growing by the moment. We were on a boat in the middle of a storm, just off the coast of Antarctica. Every single day brought with it new adventures that few men or women on earth have had the privilege of experiencing. What made it even crazier was that we were shooting a sitcom. It was ridiculous.

"I think we should go inside now!" I said as the boat slammed into yet another wave.

No one argued. We had gotten what we needed. It took a couple of minutes to brave the trek back to the main cabin, but we made it. Once safely inside we began to warm ourselves with laughter and stories of "can you believe what we just did?"

No matter how large the dream in our hearts, or whether or not we yet know what that dream may be, when we commit to doing our best with what we have, God will always be faithful to reveal our path. The point of pursuing any dream is to awaken more fully to God and to open ourselves to the experience of deeper meaning in our lives. I believe these things are tied together. When we sleep to life, we sleep in our relationship with God. When we lack magic in our lives, we lack magic in our relationship with God.

As we begin to chase our dreams, they may shift or change completely. Sometimes we will pursue one thing and God will present something else entirely, something far more exciting than our small dreams. Yet had we not pursued them in the first place, had we not run boldly forward, we never would have been in the place for God to show us those things that could truly awaken our hearts.

Awakening to life isn't about doing the big things; it's about embracing the here and now. When we do this, the "big moments" present themselves when we're ready for them. In the meantime, we simply need to do the best we can with what's in front of us.

Whenever one of my students told me they were struggling to find their purpose in life, I always asked the same question: "Are you doing the things you know you're supposed to do?" I believe this is the answer to the question of purpose. It's the "small things" that create the fertile ground for the awakened heart.

It was that small step of creating a reality show that set me on the path to eventually directing a series in Antarctica. The journey has been crazy—something I never could have predicted. It has been a journey that has kept me on the edge of my seat. The best stories are those that catch us by surprise—an unexpected beauty enters our lives; an unforeseen opportunity arises. These are the moments that bring wonder to our lives. These are the moments an awakened heart lives for.

zph.com/awake/6.5

Scan QR codes and place device here or go to zph.com/awake/6.6 and zph.com/awake/6.7

zph.com/awake/6.8

zph.com/awake/6.9

CHAPTER SEVEN

Loving Three
December 2010 China

I sprinted down the long flight of stairs into the subway system. Just before I rounded a corner I glanced back. The three men in military uniforms, as well as two undercover police officers, weren't far behind. I had two options: straight in front of me was a long passageway leading to another stairway that would take me back up to the street; to my left were turnstiles that would lead me deeper into the subway.

Hundreds of people filled the subway station, going about their daily routines as I ran full-out, doing my best to maneuver between them. I decided to take the passageway and try to get to the stairs before the officers rounded the corner behind me. I didn't know the subway enough to feel comfortable, and I couldn't read the language on any of the posted signs.

I bounded up the stairs, taking them three at a time. Once I reached the top I didn't bother looking back; I just kept running. Half a block away stood four enclosed taxi carts parked on a curb. Grabbing a fistful of coins, I thrust them at the driver of the cart at the front of the line. He was an older man with just a few long whiskers protruding from his chin.

He looked at me curiously. I was sweating and desperately trying to catch my breath. I grabbed a small map from my pocket and pointed at a specific spot. He looked at the spot, nodded, and then turned around and took off. I had no idea where we were going. I had just pointed to the first spot my finger landed on. But as long as it was away from here, that was all that mattered.

I hadn't come to China planning to do anything illegal. In fact, as far as I understand it, *I* hadn't actually done anything illegal; it was the family I was with who had broken the law. Yet here I was, running like I'd never run before and being chased by both Chinese military and the secret police.

Twenty-Four Hours Earlier

The offices of the Associated Press (AP) were impressive. The massive windows that should have offered spectacular views of the sprawling city instead showed only dense smog. We were high up in a skyscraper in the

center of Beijing, yet the smog was so thick that buildings only a block away were almost lost to sight.

I had come to the AP to tell them what we were planning. I was only a few seconds into my story when one of the reporters told me not to say another word. A minute later, I found myself sitting in a small conference room at the back of the office.

I was told that the room was swept for bugging devices several times a day, so I could be sure nobody was listening. This surprised me. Here I was in the offices of the AP, and they were concerned about being bugged?

When all the relevant reporters had arrived, I told them the story of our thirteen-year-old client, Jonathan Lee. Jonathan, who is half American and half Korean, grew up in Jackson, Mississippi. When he was ten, Jonathan had the amazing opportunity to meet President Kim Dae-jung of South Korea. In their brief conversation, Jonathan learned a little about the war between North and South Korea. Throughout my life, I've learned about many wars. At no point have I considered, even for a second, that I might play a role in stopping one of them. But when Jonathan learned about the war that has divided the Koreas for over sixty years, he decided to do something about it.

In studying the complexities of the Korean War, Jonathan quickly learned that if peace was ever going to be possible, North and South Korea, the United States, and China would each need to play a pivotal role. So, unlike any ten-year-old I've met, Jonathan wrote out a peace plan. Nobody asked him to write it; he just thought somebody needed to do something. During the period between the ages of ten and thirteen, Jonathan met with President Obama, President Kim Dae-jung (2000 Nobel Peace Prize laureate), and President Lee Myung-bak of South Korea, and he was even allowed into North Korea to meet with some of the country's top generals. These generals promised him that they would present his peace plan to North Korea's leader, Kim Jongi-il.

Yet no matter how many times Jonathan tried to meet with President Hu Jintao of China, he was turned away. And though he sent many letters, he could never get confirmation that the president had received any of them.

zph.com/awake/7.1

One night, just after Jonathan had turned thirteen, he walked into his parents' bedroom and told them what he wanted to do. Both were adamantly opposed. But he kept telling them and telling them and telling them. And as any well-honed thirteen-year-old does, Jonathan finally wore them down.

Jonathan had been learning about China, and more specifically, about Tiananmen Square. He figured that if he could stand in Tiananmen Square and hold up a banner that spoke of peace between the Koreas, as well as offer a letter that outlined his plan, just maybe the Chinese government would finally take him seriously.

This is the story I told to the reporters at the AP. This was Jonathan's plan. As I spoke, they began to look less and less impressed. The moment I finished telling of Jonathan's plan, as well as our intent to film a documentary, each reporter took turns telling me why we should give up and go home. They said that if we went through with it, at best the entire Lee family (and potentially my business partner, Nick, and I) would be deported. Then they gave me the worst-case scenario. They said that Jonathan and his family might be detained (potentially for a long time), interrogated, and then deported. If Nick and I were believed to be involved, the same thing could happen to us. Finally, they let me know it was highly possible that the Chinese government would use brutal force in shutting Jonathan down.

After hearing this, I completely agreed that the plan was too dangerous. The problem was, it wasn't *my* plan. I was simply the director hired to make the documentary. I told the reporters that I would try to talk Jonathan and his parents out of this crazy plan. However, if he was unwilling to listen, I hoped that the AP might be willing to come out and join us in telling the story. I hoped their presence might ensure that Jonathan would be in *less* trouble. When they agreed, I gave them more details and headed out.

As I was leaving, one of the reporters took me aside and told me to be careful. He said that up to one-third of the tourists in Tiananmen Square could actually be undercover police officers. He let me know that we needed to be cautious about what we said in public or in our phone conversations.

My meetings with Reuters, ABC, and CNN went much the same. I had started the day feeling carefree and like I was on the verge of a grand adventure.

I ended it feeling scared and thinking we should walk away from this project.

That evening I sat down and had a conversation with thirteen-year-old Jonathan Lee. To be honest, I was pretty sure his parents were being irresponsible, and I had decided it was time for me to step in. Jonathan and I talked in the hallway outside his hotel room.

"Jonathan, do you understand that what you are planning will more than likely mean you will never be allowed to come back to China?"

"Yes." He was more serious than he had been in days. "My parents told me that might happen."

"OK, but do you understand that the police might actually punch you? It's possible that you might be interrogated, and you may not see your family for days."

"Do you think they are going to hit me?" I could tell he was starting to get worried. "What do you think is the worst thing they will do to me?"

"I don't know. They might not do anything. They might just kick you out of the country. But you need to know that every reporter I talked to today told me that the military might also overreact and that it could get very physical."

Jonathan thought about this. Then he spoke with a quiet confidence. "I don't think God likes war. I think he wants peace between North and South Korea, and I have a plan for peace. I don't know, but I think this is the right thing to do, so I'm going to do it."

The answer Jonathan gave was the exact reason we were filming this documentary. In many ways, Jonathan is like every thirteen-year-old boy I've met. He can be annoying; he doesn't listen; he can be a pest; he fights with his little sister. He thinks farts are funny; he tells ridiculously dumb jokes; he gets embarrassed when his sister makes fun of him for liking a girl.

But Jonathan is also unlike any thirteen-year-old boy I've ever met. He understands something that many people six times his age have yet to figure out. Jonathan understands a small part of who God has called him to be.

It was because of Jonathan Lee that I found myself in Tiananmen Square in front of the Forbidden Palace in Beijing, China. After hearing his answers, I decided that if Jonathan could be this brave, the least I could do was continue with the documentary.

I arrived at the square a half hour early. I wanted to be sure I didn't miss my chance to get the best shot possible. Nick was going to arrive just five minutes before Jonathan; he was spending the morning with the family, capturing the final hours before Jonathan came to the square. Even though I was standing among thousands of people, I still felt like I stood out like a sore thumb. And I did. Although Tiananmen Square was littered with tourists, most of them were of Asian descent and a good six to twelve inches shorter than I am.

While milling around in front of the palace, I noticed a reporter I had seen in the ABC office the day before. I walked over and bent down to tie my shoe. I knew it was untied because I had just untied it a minute earlier.

"Thanks for coming," I whispered from my knee.

The man had seen me approach. Turning to look in another direction, he whispered. "I've seen Reuters, AP, and CNN in the crowd. It's crazy that they're all here."

"I know," I whispered. "This whole thing is crazy." My adrenaline was really pumping now.

With that I stood and walked away. As I made my way over to the planned location, a group of four policemen stopped me and asked to see my press credentials. They had apparently also noticed all the reporters who were pretending to be tourists. One of them must have seen me interacting with the guy from ABC. I played dumb and asked for directions to the Silk Market. In the end they let me walk away.

It was then that I saw my partner, Nick, in the crowd. If he was here, then I knew Jonathan was on his way. If everything went as planned, Jonathan Lee would be arrested, and Nick and I would slip away without the police having any idea we were involved. We had brought very small and innocent-looking cameras for exactly this reason.

Suddenly I saw Jonathan Lee. I had somehow missed the unassuming thirteen-year-old's arrival. He was just seconds away from unfurling his banner. Quickly positioning my camera, I was able to capture the event. It took exactly twenty-eight seconds for the uniformed officers and secret police to swarm around him.

In the end, the fact that Jonathan was half American and only thirteen years old played to his advantage. He wasn't tackled and kicked in the chest, as the last protester had been. He was simply escorted away, somewhat courteously. Though he was interrogated (along with his mother), it was apparently a very cordial affair. Within twelve hours, the entire Lee family was asked to leave and escorted out of the country without any major mishap. It was a much better outcome than anyone expected.

For Nick and me, the story became much crazier from the moment Jonathan and his mother were taken into custody. We had planned to split up and meet at a small pub near our hotel. The problem was that both of us were followed when we left the square. It was a truly insane few hours. Nick real-

zph.com/awake/7.2

ized he needed to change the plan. He quickly raced to the hotel, grabbed his stuff, and made a mad dash to the airport. He had all the footage, and if he didn't get it out of the country, there wouldn't be any documentary. I disappeared by means of the subway system and multiple taxis and then eventually holed myself up in my hotel room.

Nick and I both experienced a somewhat unbelievable story over the next twenty-four hours, feeling just a little like Jason Bourne. Yet in the end we both left the country safely and without incident.

I don't share this story because anything Nick or I did was impressive. We were simply doing our best to capture the story of someone who is truly impressive. When we heard about Jonathan's crazy plan, we thought it was the most naive idea in the world. Jonathan is thirteen. It is ridiculous to think he can make a difference in something as big as a war between two countries. Why would his parents let him do this? It was only after I flew down to Mississippi to meet the kid that I decided to take on this documentary project. Yes, it was a ridiculous and naive plan, but this kid was anything but ridiculous, and there was something quite beautiful about his naïveté. Besides, what truly great plan isn't ridiculous and naive?

In the end, Nick and I were able to spend three weeks with Jonathan. As we watched him, it became clear that this kid seemed to understand some things that have eluded much of the world. Jonathan has fully embraced the dreams in his heart and has risked in order to make them happen. I think this is why the kid has figured out at least some of what he has to offer this world. But what I find to be even more amazing is that Jonathan has learned how to love ... himself.

The Missing Piece

I was visiting a church recently and found myself listening to a sermon on Jesus' greatest commandment. The pastor read a verse I think I've heard more than any other verse: "Love the Lord your God with all your heart and with all your soul and with all your mind; and love your neighbor." He quoted the verse at least ten times throughout his message.

Something was annoying me, but I couldn't figure out what it was. I picked up my Bible, found the verse, and read it. I was right. The actual verse reads,

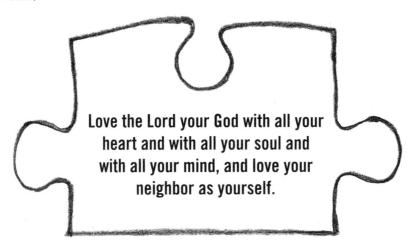

Love the Lord your God with all your heart and with all your soul and with all your mind, and love your neighbor as yourself.

The pastor is a great guy and he was preaching a good sermon. But it was as if those two little words, *"as yourself,"* got in the way of what he was trying to say. They were unimportant.

The verse is found in Matthew 22, and this entire section is amazing. Jesus speaks these words in response to some of the religious teachers of his day. Apparently there are over six hundred laws in the Old Testament. The religious leaders asked Jesus to tell them which was the most important. Jesus ignored the question and came up with two new laws that would encapsulate everything. *Love God with all you have, and love your neighbor as yourself.* Jesus broke down a thousand plus years of law into these three statements. I think this is pretty huge. It's like the CliffsNotes for life.

I just ran the numbers, and it's safe to say I've heard at least 1,800 sermons in my life. I've sat in Anglican, Baptist, Pentecostal, Southern Baptist, Methodist, Wesleyan, charismatic, nondenominational, and you-name-it churches. I've experienced God in all of them. Yet in all my years of going to church, in all my years of learning from sermons, I have only ever heard one sermon about the "as yourself" portion of this Scripture.

The message was simple. The pastor said that loving myself had something to do with eating right, going to the gym, and generally looking after myself. It meant that I should stand in front of a mirror and talk to myself, affirming those things I like about me. Even as a child I remember thinking that this was a very silly message.

If I understand language at all, *"as yourself"* is put on an equal level with *"loving your neighbor,"* just one step under *"loving God."* If this is true, then it is one of the three most important things we could ever do with our lives. Yet I understand why it's not talked about. Pride is something that nobody needs to learn. We don't need to be taught to think highly of ourselves; it is humility that's the hard lesson. I'm sure this is why we spend most of our time learning how to love God and love others.

If anything, it would be easy to look at the world and say we all love ourselves too much. With much of the world obsessed with making more money and buying the newest "toys," it would make sense to say we need to learn to teach, teach, teach people how to live outside themselves and spend time loving their neighbors. But excess and pride have nothing to do with love. And no one needs teaching on how to overindulge or be self-centered. No one needs to learn how to consider themselves more important than someone else. Unfortunately, this comes naturally to most of us. Yet these things have nothing to do with love.

I think the reason for much of the excess and egotism in the world is precisely that we haven't taken the time to learn how to love ourselves. It is in loving ourselves that we learn humility. It is in loving ourselves that we begin to understand that excess isn't the answer. And most important, it is in loving ourselves that we are able to fully love others.

I no longer think that breaking down Jesus' second greatest commandment into healthy eating, exercise, and positive self-esteem is what Jesus was talking about. Although he doesn't spell it out for us precisely, I think that when Jesus told us to love ourselves, he was commanding us to live fully awake.

We can't truly love someone unless we know them. True intimate love by its very nature is specific and personal. If I want to love my wife, I must know her. I must be willing to sacrifice in a way that specifically touches her heart. When I do this, she awakens to my love in a greater measure.

When I hear that Jesus loved me so much that he died for me, I understand as a Christian that this is at the heart of what I believe and who I am. Yet Jesus didn't just die for "the world," and he didn't just conquer "all" sin. He died for *me* specifically, and when he conquered sin, he conquered *my* sin, specifically. Because he did this with me in mind, because he loved me specifically, my heart has been awakened by his love.

Love is specific. Love without actions or sacrifice is not love. Love is targeted. If I am going to show someone I love them, I need to know what I can do that will help to awaken his or her heart.

Yet when I ask people if they know how to love themselves, they are often confused and think it's a trick question. But I don't think it's too hard. A while back I wrote out a few questions that helped me define what it means to love myself.

The Loving Questions

- What are the things that make me come alive?
- What awakens my heart and sets my mind to dreaming?
- What captures my imagination?
- What experiences bring me closer to beauty, wonder, and magic, closer to God?

I think a major part of our journey has to do with finding the answers to these questions. As the years pass, our answers will shift and change. There will always be seasons in which these questions feel far away or even irrelevant, yet they are always important. We are *commanded* to love ourselves.

I believe one of the key ways God shows his love to us is through the opportunities he gives us to awaken our hearts. Each time I step out in faith and embrace life to its fullest, I awaken to a deeper intimacy in my relationship with Jesus. I believe the way we most fully experience God's love is when

Scan QR code and place device here or go to zph.com/awake/7.3

we make the choice to love ourselves enough to pursue what he has placed in front of us.

When we are fully awake, experiencing God in our hearts, in the beauty surrounding our stories, in our imaginations, and in our dreams, love is the natural outflow. When we are fully awake, even the impossibly hard choices become easier to make.

Jonathan Lee

Spending a month with Jonathan Lee was exhausting. Jonathan is thirteen. Thirteen-year-olds aren't supposed to have anything figured out. No one expects much from their kind. In fact, I usually just feel bad for them. It seems like thirteen is God's big joke—hormones rage, zits sprout, and everything is awkward and gangly.

Yet somehow, in the midst of living a story that could literally get the kid beaten up, ripped away from his family, and thrown into a cell, Jonathan was able to keep his heart awake to the beauty, magic, and wonder around him. He never took himself too seriously or considered his "mission" overly important. Jonathan made time to laugh and crack jokes and go to the Beijing Lego store. He found the time to pull pranks on his little sister and dream of what the future might bring. In Beijing, away from his normal life, these are some of the things that awakened Jonathan's heart.

I don't know if this is something Jonathan has learned or if it just comes with the territory of being thirteen. Regardless, it was amazing to watch. I spent hours trying to scare the kid. I wanted him to fully understand the gravity of his choices. I wanted him to realize that life isn't all pranks and fart jokes. Yet somehow Jonathan was able to see the risk in front of him and do his best to understand it. Then, in the moments between the intense and hard choices of his life, Jonathan was able to love himself. And I believe it was this love that allowed him to make confident decisions to love others.

Young Jonathan Lee stepped up to the plate in a way that many people much older than him would struggle to do. He had a dream for peace, and though he has yet to achieve it, he has not given up. As Jonathan grows, so too will his wisdom and his impact, but for now, he is doing the best he can with what he has, and in the moments between, he's not trying to be all grown-up about it.

Jonathan loves himself. He doesn't need anyone to tell him that he needs to laugh. He doesn't feel guilty or immature for craving wonder and beauty. His faith is childlike, yet he is a young man. I pray he will not lose this faith as he grows older.

Jesus talks about childlike faith in the Bible. I think a big reason is that most children don't have a problem dreaming and laughing. But then the child grows up. He or she gets married, has kids, and buys a house. Growing up becomes the entirety of not just who they are but why they are. It is easy for grown-ups to forget that laughter and whimsy are the best medicine for even the hardest moments in life. Many of the grown-ups I know seem to be unaware of the beauty and wonder available to them on a daily basis—both in the good times as well as the bad.

Like Jonathan Lee, I want to stand up for what's important and communicate value for people when it matters most. I want to make the hard choices when I need to make them. Just as Jonathan frolicked among the Legos, I want to be able to experience joy in the midst of all of my circumstances. And just like Jonathan, when I have a dream in my heart, I want to take steps toward realizing it.

I think this is what living with a childlike faith looks like.

CHAPTER EIGHT

Anywhere on the Planet
April 2004 South Africa

It was midnight when the call came.

"Hello," I heard Nick say into his phone. "Hello. Linda, is that you?" Nick looked at his phone in confusion. He dialed a number and waited.

"Come on!" He hung up and tried the number yet again.

I looked up from my computer. "What's going on?"

"Linda just called. All I heard was an urgent whispering, and then the phone went dead." Without another word, he ran off to find his fiancée, Heather.

Just four days earlier, Nick, Heather, and I had been at Linda's house. Linda is Heather's mom. We had spent most of the weekend cleaning up pools of blood, ripping out bloody carpets, and installing new security gates. Linda lived alone on a large property about forty miles outside of Johannesburg. She had bought the property to use as a place to love hurting people. Some were addicts, some survivors of abuse, and some ex-convicts. These individuals, usually broken, came to her "camp" for prayer and healing, and they found it there.

Linda's friend—a man in his midforties—had been murdered in her living room. She had been sleeping upstairs when the brutal murder took place. The man and his two teenage boys had been staying in her house on the ground floor. It was a great arrangement. The man and his kids had a place to stay, and he was able to help with the security of the property. That night, a burglar entered the premises and grabbed their TV. The man woke up to a strange sound and went to see what was happening. Without a second thought, the burglar shot the man three times in the chest, killing him instantly. He killed the man for a TV.

The man's two boys were sleeping over at a friend's house on the night their father was murdered. They wouldn't find out about his death until the next morning. When they arrived, his body had already been taken away, but the police were still in the house, and their father's blood was everywhere. The oldest boy was fifteen, and his little brother was twelve. Both boys' lives were changed in an instant. Both of them lived through more loss in that moment than many experience in a lifetime.

The police told Linda that a gang had been terrorizing the area. They said that her friend was the seventeenth murder over the past two weeks and that more than one burglar had likely been involved. They encouraged her to get a security system and install thick security gates throughout the house.

The night Linda called with an urgent whisper was another sobering moment. When Nick called her back, her cell went straight to voice mail. When Heather tried the landline, she realized it had either been unplugged or the line had been cut. Linda lived a full half hour from us. All three of us ran to the car. It took seventeen minutes to make that drive. Nick hit multiple curbs, and I swear he had all four wheels off the ground at least once. On the way over, Heather called the police. There was a police station only ten minutes from Linda's home, and we were hoping they could get there sooner.

Linda's property fills just over sixty acres and is surrounded by a large spiked fence that stands seven feet tall. The fence was a deterrent, but there were still a number of places where someone could squeeze under it. There was no lighting anywhere on the fence except at the front gate. When you arrive at the gate, you are supposed to push a button that rings the phone at the house. Once the gate is opened, it is a three- or four-acre drive through the tree-lined driveway leading to the house.

As we drove to the gate, I jumped out of the car to push the button. It was dark, and I couldn't see it at first. Eventually my hand found the button, and it was obvious that someone had destroyed it. Nick and Heather got out of the car, and we all stood at the fence for a moment, helpless. The police still hadn't arrived, and we couldn't even see the house from where we were standing. I started to climb the fence.

"What are you doing?" Heather's whisper sounded urgent. Nick saw what I was doing and immediately joined me. It took me a moment to figure out how to jump over the spikes and onto the property without impaling my-self or breaking an ankle as I landed. I leaped over the top spike from my hunched position, and I heard my jeans rip loudly. I hit the ground hard, but other than the torn jeans, I was OK.

"Nick, Joel, stop it!" Heather called out tearfully as Nick plummeted to the ground behind me. We both stood on the other side of the fence, only now realizing that we had left Heather alone in the dark.

"Get in the car and drive to the police station and see what the hell is taking them so long," Nick whispered back to his fiancée.

"What do you think you guys are going to be able to do?" Heather was pan-icked. "You don't have guns or anything."

There was a definite pause as Nick and I looked at each other, both of us uncertain about how to answer.

"Just go!" Nick whispered. Heather jumped into the car and drove away, shooting a final, frantic look back at Nick before she disappeared into the night.

zph.com/awake/8.1

Nick and I immediately started walking down the long, dark driveway. For the first thirty seconds or so, we were both so hyped on adrenaline that we didn't think about anything other than getting to Linda. As we walked further down the dark driveway, reality began to sink in. We began to think through the choice we had made. More than likely, there was a man, or multiple men, with guns waiting at the end of the driveway.

As we rounded a corner, the house came into view. It was shrouded in darkness, the only light coming from a dim bulb above the front door. This was the moment reality came crashing down. Until now, my adrenaline had muted my fear. Now, I suddenly felt like that stupid girl in the horror films. We knew there was a killer loose, yet we had still decided to go for our walk through the creepy forest.

We crouched low and quietly made our way over to a woodpile off to our left. We were still at least a couple hundred feet from the house. As we peeked from behind the pile, we saw the shape of a large, hulking figure standing in the shadow of the door. We couldn't see the figure clearly and were too far away to know if it was human or simply a trick of the light.

"So what do we do now?" Nick whispered.

This is where our plan ended. Yet I knew we couldn't turn back, and by the resolve in Nick's eyes I could see he agreed with me.

"OK," I said, "I'm going to run over to the other side of the house. I'll go wide so I won't be seen. When I'm directly on the other side, I'll stand and scream 'Police' at the top of my lungs. When I do that, you stand up on this side and do the same."

Nick nodded, clearly seeing the genius of my plan.

"When they hear our voices coming from two different directions, they'll think there are a lot more of us, and they'll run."

When I finished saying "and they'll run," we both looked at each other, realizing that this was, in fact, a very stupid plan. Nick nodded, and without another word I ran into the darkness.

Tea Time

"This is the police!" I screamed at the top of my lungs.

"This is the—" I heard from the other side of the house. Nick's voice was surprisingly more like a woman's than I remembered. He stopped and screamed again, this time in his usual, manly tone. "This is the police!" he screamed.

I began taking slow steps toward the house, screaming the whole time. I remember realizing that the police probably would have had flashlights and definitely would have had guns. Both of us were screaming louder as we approached. The hulking figure we had seen in the doorway was gone. That scared me more than anything.

No shots had been fired, and no screams of rage were coming from the house. As we came close to the doorway, I had a very clear thought pop into my head. "They are waiting for the two idiots without weapons to walk up to the door so they can shoot us, point-blank."

Eventually I could see Nick. We both came around the corner, walking toward each other and still screaming. I could see confusion and fear in Nick's face, which I knew clearly mirrored my own. We were almost next to each other now, directly opposite the front door and still screaming loudly. Out of nowhere a high-pitched voice interrupted us.

"Well, hello, boys, what in the world are you doing here?"

Both of us jumped in fear, spinning around to see where the voice had come from. We didn't see anyone.

"Boys, what are you doing? It's almost one in the morning. Do you want some tea?" By the end of the question, we had both looked up to see Linda standing in her nightgown at the bedroom window. She looked confused and very motherly.

Heather and the police came a few minutes later. We all had a good laugh about just how stupid we had been. Linda hadn't meant to call Nick; she must have dialed him by mistake just before she turned off her phones for the night. She apparently always unplugs her landline at night because people call her all the time.

The police apologized for taking so long and promised to do better the next time. It was funny and incredibly scary, and we laughed so hard that we cried.

After we left, Linda had trouble going back to sleep. After an hour or more of lying in bed, she was still wide-awake. If she hadn't been so wide-awake, she never would have heard the men with the bolt cutters who were busy disassembling the newly installed security gate at her front door.

For the second time that night, Linda stuck her head out the window. She was surprised to see six armed men standing boldly in the light of the moon. She immediately found her phone and called Nick and then called the police. Next she took out her shofar (an old-fashioned ram's horn) and stood at the window and blew it. I honestly have no idea what she was thinking here, but who am I to question Linda's tactics? She also turned on some worship music and blared it out the window at the men. Not surprisingly, even with the horn and the worship music, the gang was unafraid. When Linda showed no fear, the men began screaming and cursing at her, telling her that they were coming for her. From the momentary safety of her window she watched as they took out three sledgehammers and went to work knocking down her door.

This time, the police did arrive in record time. It took them twelve minutes where before it had taken a full hour. Having just been there an hour earlier, they knew exactly where to go and had given us their word they would take a special interest in Linda. They were the first to arrive and chase the men away.

Commands, Part 2

Jesus commanded us to love our neighbors *as ourselves*. I love myself a lot. This is a heavy command. The reality is that no matter what kind of dangerous, painful, or hard circumstance I find myself in, I would be happy for any neighbor anywhere on the planet to step into my world and offer help. I love myself that much. And yet there have been multiple occasions when I've chosen *not* to love my neighbor. In the story above, however, Nick and I embraced the opportunity to step into the unknown and love Linda with our actions.

In the first chapter of this book, I tell the story about seeing a woman attacked in Haiti. When I tell people I feel guilty about not helping the woman, they often tell me that I was "wise" to not help her. But that's not right. Wisdom means loving my neighbor *as myself*. If I were being attacked, anywhere, I would very much want someone to try to help me. That woman was my neighbor. When we thought Linda was in trouble, the question wasn't "What if they have guns?" but "What would I need if I were in her situation?" Loving my neighbor *as myself* is a heavy command.

My desire in life is to live fully awake. I don't want to miss an opportunity to find God and experience him. But I don't believe it's possible to live awake unless we've learned how to love God and love our neighbor *as ourselves*. Those two little words are a lot bigger than we give them credit for.

Luke 10:29 records this question posed to Jesus by an expert in the law: "Who is my neighbor?" Jesus responds by telling him a story about a man who was beaten and thrown down on the street. It was just some random guy who got beat up—a guy no one knew. Jesus went on to explain that this man is a great example of "our neighbor"—just some random guy. To love my neighbor as myself is not an easy command. It borders on the insane. And if Jesus wasn't cracking a joke, I apparently have close to seven billion neighbors.

Johannesburg, Five Years Later

Five years later, on the very same property, Linda, Heather, and Nick would experience an unimaginable tragedy. I wasn't with them when this story played out. I was out of the country and only heard about it in an e-mail from Nick a few days later.

Something quite tragic just happened. This Thursday around midnight I got a call from my mother-in-law. She told me she had been visiting with her friend Emily and her two young daughters. In the middle of the visit, two heavily armed men entered the house.

When Emily saw the men, she tried to escape with her two daughters. In a desperate panic, she and her daughters ran outside and jumped into their car. Putting it in reverse, she tried to drive away. She was frantic, both of her girls screaming in the backseat. Before she could get away, Emily slammed into a tree.

The men charged the car, still firing, and she was struck multiple times. She died instantly. There was no reason for this violence. It was a brutal, unjustified act.

When we got the call, we drove straight to the hospital. I saw Emily's husband, coated in her blood and weeping at his loss. I saw her two daughters. They were clearly in shock, unable to comprehend what had just happened . . .

—Nick

Nick was angry. Heather was angry and scared. The husband was desperate with grief, and his daughters were beyond traumatized. They would grow up without a mother, and they would grow up without answers.

There are over fifty murders a day in South Africa, most of them violent. People around the world can't understand this statistic. The more recent wars of America don't even come close. Fifty murders a day. This means that every single day, fifty families are left without answers, and this is just in South Africa. This means that, every day, fifty families are desperately in need of love.

zph.com/awake/8.2

The Case for Love

As a filmmaker, I've spent a large part of my career creating commercials and documentaries that focus on some awfully horrid things. My company has produced films about the issues of child slavery in Haiti, kidnapping, HIV/AIDS, forced early marriage, the orphan crisis in Africa, and more. My beautiful wife has spent most of her career working on the issues of HIV/AIDS, human trafficking, gender inequality, and extreme poverty.

There is horrible injustice in our world. I've spent much of the last few years witnessing it firsthand. I've met countless men, women, and children all over the world who have suffered in ways that I can't begin to imagine. I have wept with some of them as they shared their stories. I used to search for the right words to help bring meaning to their suffering. I used to think there was such a thing as "the right words."

I remember sitting with a young girl in Haiti as we interviewed her for one of our documentaries. She was only fifteen, and she had been a slave for the past nine years. Her "owner" beat and raped her on a daily basis. She wore her scars on her body and on her soul. There were no words to speak that would have made an ounce of difference.

In Zambia, I spent time with a thirteen-year-old girl who was forced to marry an eighty-year-old man. Her parents had sold her to the man for a few dollars.

In Cambodia, my wife works with women who have been sold as sex slaves. Many of them have been forced to sleep with men up to twenty times a day for many years. Let me write that again. Many of these women have been forced to sleep with men up to twenty times a day for many years. Some of these "women" are as young as four years old.

Recently I spent time in rural Mozambique in a village that has more orphans than adults. Over half of the adults in the village have died from easily treatable diseases, as well as from HIV/AIDS. These deaths have left a generation of children with no one to look after them.

I could go on for many more pages. I have seen with my own eyes atrocities that have left me speechless, tragedies that have broken my heart. When

zph.com/awake/8.3

zph.com/awake/8.4

I hear about poverty or injustice, I see the names and faces of countless people I have come to know over the years. Just as I've come to learn that not for a second is any human on the planet more than a step away from beauty and wonder, I also understand that not for a single second is any human on the planet more than a step away from tragedy and pain. If this is true, then how can I spend so much time talking about life being magical, whimsical, and beautiful?

Neighbors

I don't need to leave the United States to find horror and pain. Just a few days ago, my wife and I were driving down the street in Washington, D.C., where we now live. As we rounded a corner, we saw a homeless man sleeping on the sidewalk. When we saw the man, my amazing, compassionate wife burst into tears. We stopped and gave him a blanket from the back of our car. He woke up long enough to thank us and then rolled over and went back to sleep.

This man was my neighbor. And though I gave him a blanket, I still don't think I loved him "as myself." If I'm being honest, if I were him, I'd have wanted a place to stay or maybe some company and a hot meal. I'd have wanted to share my story and make a friend.

zph.com/awake/8.5

"Practical Reasons NOT to Love the Homeless" List

1. What about the issue of self-responsibility? This man might have chosen to do the wrong thing. Maybe he chose to walk out on his life.

2. What about safety? This guy could have robbed me.

3. What about my finances? Can I even afford to take the man out for dinner?

4. I'm not sure I have the time to "love" this man. If I do this, am I going to stop for every homeless man in D.C.? I'll go broke myself!

5. How do I know this guy isn't a con artist? I read about that family of "beggars" who make $250,000 a year.

It's the words *if I were him* that throw me off. I think that loving someone "as yourself" implies that we put ourselves into his or her shoes and ask, "If I were him or her, what would awaken my soul? If I were him or her, what would I need to truly feel loved?" The problem is, the moment I ask this question, a massive list of new questions immediately comes to mind.

Once I make it this far down my list, I usually realize that my thoughts about helping this man were highly impractical. In fact, I find it pretty easy not to love the homeless *as myself.* It often even feels like the responsible choice.

But what about the kids in my neighborhood who are growing up without a father? There are a few places where my wife and I have thought about volunteering as mentors. Could I try to love them as myself?

It's usually at about this point when I realize that it is very impractical to love the kids in my neighborhood.

I could easily continue. It doesn't matter who my neighbor is. I've got a great list for almost every scenario. I've got more "neighbors" than I could ever hope to love. And this is where my answer lies; this is where I get off the hook. With so much pain just outside my front door, let alone the world, how can I be expected to do anything about it? I only have so much time in my day, and I've got dreams of my own.

I believe that when we love God and allow our hearts to be awakened by his love, we will also be awakened with a deep desire to see justice in our world. For when we live awake, God's desires become our desires; his dreams become our dreams.

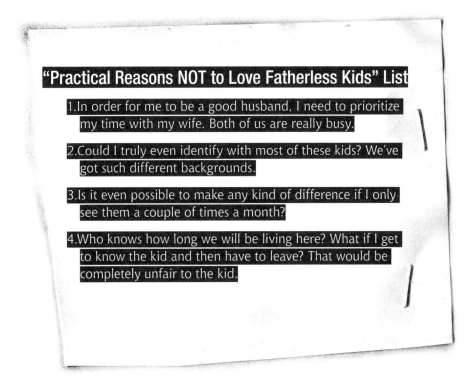

"Practical Reasons NOT to Love Fatherless Kids" List

1. In order for me to be a good husband, I need to prioritize my time with my wife. Both of us are really busy.

2. Could I truly even identify with most of these kids? We've got such different backgrounds.

3. Is it even possible to make any kind of difference if I only see them a couple of times a month?

4. Who knows how long we will be living here? What if I get to know the kid and then have to leave? That would be completely unfair to the kid.

It's easy to hear the story of the priest in Haiti and think, "That's amazing." But when I encounter one homeless man, the excuses pile on. I've begun to wonder if my excuses are the reason many of my "neighbors" are experiencing some kind of heartache or pain. I've begun to think that my justifications might be one of the reasons evil is running rampant and there is desperate poverty and injustice in the world.

What Pleasure Feels Like, Part 2

Just as we all must learn specific ways to love ourselves, we also must learn how we were designed to love others. The way I was created to love won't be the way you were created to love. And just as we learn how to love ourselves by taking every opportunity to awaken our hearts, I think this is also how we learn to love others. Each time we step out and love someone with our actions, we further define who we are meant to be in this world.

Over the years, I've come to learn that I love to mentor the next generation. I love working with high school students who've grown up without a father, who have lacked guidance in some way. I love breaking a sweat as I physically work alongside someone who needs my help. I love to step into broken relationships and try to bring restoration. These are some of the ways I was created to love. When I love in these ways, I feel God's pleasure.

I don't get excited when I volunteer in a soup kitchen or mentor young children. My heart isn't awakened when I join a community group and clean up the neighborhood. I don't love visiting hospitals or senior citizens homes. This doesn't mean I don't do these things from time to time, but rather that I focus on the ways I was created to love. If I try to love like the priest or like my wife, I will quickly become burned-out and unable to continue. But when I learn the actions of love that awaken my soul, love becomes what it was always meant to be—an amazing adventure, as well as something that I actually desire to do.

Earlier in this chapter, I wrote about some of the most atrocious horrors I've seen in my life—murder, sex trafficking, forced early marriages, a parentless generation, and so forth. I believe that much of the horror and pain in our world is the result of a world that is sound asleep and feeling empty. It's not that we don't know the right things; it's that the right things feel like an immense sacrifice. But when we awaken to the fullness of God, when our lives are filled with wonder, beauty, and magic, when we take every opportunity to learn how to love God, the world, and ourselves, a natural outflow will be a world that experiences love.

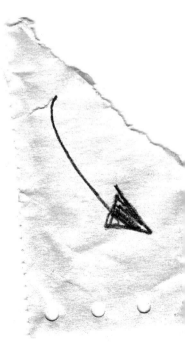

CHAPTER NINE

Get Rid of the Ashes
october 2004 South Africa

I can't believe she e-mailed me.

This thought played over and over in my head. I knew I was feeling something, but I couldn't name it. I now understand it was sheer panic. I was sitting in my car, staring forward. I didn't see anything, though I'm sure my eyes were wide-open. I just sat there, my hand outstretched, resting on the ignition. I didn't start the car. I wasn't planning on going anywhere. I was too shocked to move.

"What are you thinking?" I said aloud. "Really? You're contacting me now?" Her e-mail was brief:

> I like your website. I'm coming to Johannesburg for work. When I called your mom, she said she didn't have your number, but she gave me your website. Do you want to have coffee while I'm there? I hope to see you again.
>
> —Megan

I hadn't heard from her in approximately 1,460 days. Four years earlier, she'd broken my heart for the second time, and it had taken at least two full years before I could throw away her pictures.

Over the past year, I had met a wonderful girl. She was the only girl I'd ever met who made me forget about Megan. For the first time in years, I felt like I was able to move on. We dated for a while and had a great time together. After seven wonderful months, I called my brother.

"Dude, I'm going to do it!" My stomach fluttered with excitement.

"It's about time," Jason said. "I've been telling you for years now how good you'd look with a shaved head."

Choosing to ignore his jest, I continued. "I just bought a ring, and I'm going to propose tomorrow night!"

"DUDE!" He was truly excited now. "I can't believe it! You finally did it. We all knew it would happen eventually. I can't wait to meet her!"

I hung up the phone more excited than I had been in years. The following night, I proposed. To my amazement, she said yes, and over the next couple of months we spent a lot of time looking for wedding venues, talking through invitation lists, and dreaming of our future together.

On the day I received Megan's e-mail, everything changed. I didn't want it to. I was deeply confused that I felt any emotions at all. But reading her short message felt like holding a deadly viper.

"How is it that this woman can still have any hold on me?" This thought kept spinning through my head.

I told my fiancée that Megan was coming to town, and I thought I might want to have coffee with her. By this time I hadn't seen or heard from her in over four years. For all I knew, she was married with two kids and a cocker spaniel. My fiancée, being a lot more secure than I was, told me that I should go.

We had arranged to meet over lunch. I remember driving into the parking lot and getting out of the car. I checked my hair and was immediately irritated that I would think to check my hair. I couldn't believe how pathetic I was. I'd barely even thought of Megan for over a year, yet after a single e-mail, my insides felt like jelly. As I turned a corner, I saw her walking toward me. She spotted me about the same time.

"Joel! How are you? It's so great to see you!" Megan ran over and gave me a quick hug.

"I'm great. Wow, it's been a long time! I can't believe you're here."

And I couldn't. For more years than I care to admit, all I had ever wanted was to see Megan standing in front of me. Now here she was, but it was all wrong. Everything was wrong.

I ordered the biggest steak the restaurant had on its menu. Megan was a vegetarian, so I asked the waiter to make it extra bloody. I was determined to let her know that she held no sway over me. She was determined to eat a meal and catch up on old times.

And just like that, once again, like that first moment at summer camp more than nine years earlier, everything changed.

I spent a long time trying to forget that lunch, but no matter what I did, I couldn't get Megan out of my head or my heart. I had no idea if she actually liked me or whether I would ever contact her again, but I could see that I definitely shouldn't be getting married.

From here, the story takes a number of both terrible and lovely turns that exceed the bounds of this book. I made some awful choices that hurt both Megan and my fiancée. After a couple of months of confusion and pain, I finally called off the wedding. If you care to know a little more of the story, you can find it at the link on the next page.

STEP 1: EYE CONTACT

zph.com/awake/9.1

STEP 2: EXTEND ARMS

Ten Years, Eight Months, Thirteen Days, Eighteen Hours

Exactly eight months later, I found myself standing on the terrace of the Kennedy Center in Washington, D.C. In front of me was the beautiful Megan. I stuttered and stammered out my proposal. It is one of the most amazing moments of my life. I must have been quite poetic indeed, for when I asked her, Megan began to tear up. She didn't hesitate. She said yes, and then, right there on the top of the Kennedy Center, we created our very first signature hug.

In March 2006, we were married.

STEP 3:
WRAP &
LIFT

STEP 4:
ACCEPT
DEAD
WEIGHT

In the end, it took me ten years, eight months, thirteen days, and eighteen hours to finally get Megan to marry me. She has been the woman of my dreams since I was eighteen. From the very moment I saw her at camp, from the very moment she touched my arm and drew little circles on it, I was head over heels in love.

The Radical

When I married Megan, I knew she had a heart for justice and equality. She had been passionate about them since the day we met, but I didn't understand the extent of her passion. Megan pours out her life for the poorest and most broken people in this world. She advocates for those who have no

Scan QR code and place device here or go to zph.com/awake/9.2

one to speak for them. She loves God, others, and herself in a way I never thought possible. All of these things together make Megan even more beautiful, for these are ingredients in the recipe for a fully awakened heart.

It was just after the recent earthquake in Haiti that Megan taught me something. It was then that I began to understand the implications of Jesus' greatest commandment.

January 2010 — Haiti

On January 12, 2010, a 7.0-magnitude earthquake wreaked havoc on Haiti. From the moment we heard about the quake, Megan and I spent most of our time trying to find out if our friends were OK. We also were desperate to get there and see if we could help in any way. No commercial flights were landing in Port-au-Prince so we decided to drive to Haiti. We had yet to hear anything from most of our friends there, though I had heard some great news just six days after the earthquake. My friend Jean Marc sent me this e-mail:

> Dear Joel, God saved our lives miraculously. My house fell on top of my family, but they were all saved. I have lost everything. I have saved only what I was wearing. Thanks to God! Keep praying for us. I lost several members of my extended family, a lot of members from our church, and tons of friends. God is good.
>
> —Jean Marc

Megan had received a few e-mails that were not as encouraging. At the time, she was working with World Hope International (WHI), which supports over 48,000 orphans and vulnerable children, as well as cares for thousands of people living with HIV/AIDS in Haiti. Hundreds of orphans were missing and feared dead. There were no words to speak at a time like this. I planned on spending the next couple of weeks documenting the work WHI was doing and telling the story of what happened. Megan would be assessing the situation and planning the best way forward with WHI's Haitian leadership.

We were going to Haiti because it was the only place in the world Megan wanted to be. From the moment the earthquake struck, she was desperate to head there and do what she does best—fight for justice.

January 2010 — Dominican Republic/Haitian Border

The Dominican Republic/Haitian border was insane. Thousands of refugees were trying to get out of Haiti as hundreds of relief workers and foreign military personnel were trying to get in. When we arrived, we met up with Larousse, one of World Hope International's Haitian staff members. He was waiting for us at the border and was going to drive us into Port-au-Prince. We never handed over our passports or talked to an official. We simply flashed our USAID badges, and that was enough to allow us to drive through the chaos and into the country.

I had talked with Larousse many times, both in the United States and in Haiti, but this was different. He was cordial but otherwise quiet and missing his usual easy laugh.

"How long before your kids can go back to school?" I asked him. I was searching for something to fill the silence. I had heard that Larousse's immediate family was alive, so I thought it was a good question. It took him a moment to answer. He looked slightly confused by the question.

"Eighty percent of the schools in Port-au-Prince have been destroyed," he said. "Those that aren't destroyed are currently housing thousands of refugees. I can't imagine we will reopen schools for quite some time—years maybe."

Silence hung for a few minutes as we processed what Larousse had just said. I tried asking a couple more questions before I finally gave up. Every answer I received was soaked in loss and pain, and every answer left me speechless.

The farther we drove the more obvious it became that the news hadn't been overdramatized. Though many houses and places of business were still standing, the numbers of those that were down were staggering. Most of them weren't just "down"; they were nothing but massive piles of rubble.

Larousse was still in shock. I think most of Haiti was still in shock. Men and women walked the streets, selling their wares as children ran alongside cars, begging for food. A few stalls had been set up in an impromptu marketplace that sprouted up along the side of the road. Smoke rose from multiple

zph.com/awake/9.3

cooking fires so that a haze blanketed everything. There was a general milling around of people who were trying to carry on some semblance of life,
but over it all hung an anxiety and fear that made the air feel fragile.

Megan spent much of the drive trying to make Larousse laugh. She even suc-
ceeded a few times. She has always been great in these kinds of situations.
She knows how to engage people, no matter where they are in life. She loves
people truly and completely. Megan is like the priest in this way. She loves

with actions and yet she somehow manages to carry a tenderness mixed with her fierce love. I love that woman!

A few hours after we arrived, I found myself walking through a tent city. Thousands upon thousands of men, women, and children surrounded me. The children knew only a few words in English. Those words were enough to break my heart.

"Sir, I am hungry. Please help me?"

"Do you ... have ... food, please?"

"Please, I am hungry."

"I need water. Please help!"

There were adults around me as well. They weren't begging. They looked lost. In their eyes I saw something infinitely more tragic than hunger—I saw a loss of hope. They had lost everything; in an instant, family members, friends, their homes, livelihoods, and all of their belongings had been completely destroyed. This "camp" was one of the hundreds that sprouted throughout the city and one of the thousands that have sprouted throughout Haiti.

Just a few hours after I left the tent city, I was standing atop a massive pile of rubble that used to be the Caribbean Market. It's hard now to imagine this once-grand shopping center that should have been filled with men, women, and children pushing carts and selecting food. In my mind I could see a little girl running down the aisle with a candy bar in hand, pleading with her mother to buy it. I could see an old woman taking her time to pick out the perfect piece of fruit from the produce pile, as well as the cashier who kept checking her watch, waiting for her shift to end so she could go home and get ready for her big date. I could see all these beautiful people unaware of the beast about to roar.

As I filmed, my friend and translator from previous trips to Haiti told the story of the Caribbean Market. "Over five hundred people were inside when the earthquake struck. They are all dead now." Wisner's voice was hard and flat.

Wisner had barely survived the quake. Both of his businesses were completely destroyed, and his wife, Gardeen, is a living miracle. I still can't fathom anyone living through what she did. Two of the people who were standing next to her when the earth shuddered and groaned were buried beneath the rubble. Somehow Gardeen had been able to tunnel her way out.

I climbed to the top of this mountain of rubble. Beneath me, locked inside this mass of concrete and rebar were at least five hundred bodies. As I struggled to find my balance, the smell engulfed me. Men and women stood nearby with masks or pieces of cloth covering their faces to keep out the stench of death. As I positioned my camera, I looked closely at those who lingered in this place. I wondered if their family members were trapped inside, and if so, if they would ever be found. It was then that I had the revelation that the bodies lying beneath me were going to be trapped there for months, if not years. The devastation was so vast that there was no way to clean it up and rebuild quickly.

There were also men digging with shovels. They were no longer looking for loved ones; they had given up that hope days ago. Now they were looking for whatever they could find—something they might be able to sell so they could buy food. Others were looking for anything that might have survived the quake, something that would help them remember the lives they had lost just a couple of weeks earlier.

As I dropped to one knee and positioned my camera to film this horrid scene of debris intermingled with lost humanity, I began to notice that some of the men and woman were looking at me in

zph.com/awake/9.5

frustration. It was obvious that I hadn't earned the right to stand among them. My camera felt more like mockery than help. A large, shirtless man stood just a few steps away. The cloth that covered his nose and mouth did nothing to hide the anger that burned in his eyes. I didn't turn on my camera; I couldn't. Instead I aimed it at the ground and did my best to meet the man's eyes. After a moment, I nodded to the man and then made my way back to the car.

Every hundred feet or so, Wisner would pull over and give an update on how many men, women, and children had died inside yet another ruined building. Just moments after we left the Caribbean Market, we stopped by a secondary school that had disintegrated with almost three hundred students inside, kids who had been reading books, listening to lectures, and gossiping in the hallways. Nothing remained but a pile of rubble. I could tell that before the earthquake it had been three stories high; now it barely came up to my waist. The walls that held the thick slabs of ceiling and floor had collapsed, falling straight down.

Next we came to a Catholic girls' school that had crumbled with over 250 girls inside—beautiful girls who had made the sign of the cross over their hearts moments before the ground erupted. There are some things I simply do not understand.

Later that night, as Megan and I were lying on the ground in the dark, we did our best to talk through what we had been experiencing.

"I gave toothpaste and other health and sanitary supplies to the staff today," Megan said. "I didn't think it would be a big deal. They were so grateful." Megan's voice was breaking. "I really didn't realize just how much our staff people were lacking. They've lost everything."

zph.com/awake/9.6

"As I was walking through one of the tent cities," I said, "a young man in his midtwenties ran up to me. I recognized him but couldn't place him. It turns out that he was in one of our commercials a few years ago. As we talked, he told me that his mother had been his last living relative. When the earthquake struck, he was outside her house. He watched as it collapsed on her. A few days later, he was able to find some friends to help him dig out her body. The guy was clearly in shock and had nothing but the clothes on his back."

Megan spoke again. "The men in the tent cities have started sleeping during the day because at night men come and raid the tents and rape the women. The men in the tents are now standing guard all night."

"I just met a kid on the street who couldn't have been more than ten," I said. "He was standing in front of a pile of rubble. I took his picture and showed it to him. He smiled. I asked him what he was doing there, and he told me that his parents both died when his house fell down. He just stared at what used to be the house and said, "Now I have nowhere to go.""

Our conversation went on like this, one story leading into the next—each story as tragic as the one before.

While in Haiti, I spent my days filming some of the relief work World Hope was doing. Megan spent her days literally fighting for people's lives. One of the more memorable situations she faced that week was particularly troubling. There was a tent city in Leogane (a city about an hour and a half from the capital) where infants had begun to die of dehydration and malnutrition. The day after Megan had personally witnessed this horror, she lobbied the United Nations to ensure that the necessary formula would reach the makeshift clinic responsible for serving the infants in Leogane. Thirty hours and several meetings later, the formula arrived.

Everywhere we went, people were literally dying in front of our eyes. Families were starving all around us; people were missing; limbs were amputated; mangled bodies were being dug out of the rubble.

What Truly Matters

Every life will encounter heartache, pain, and misery from time to time. But what happened in Haiti was beyond any misery we've felt in the West. What happened in Haiti carries with it a suffering and anguish that is almost beyond belief. Mothers and fathers forced to watch their children starve; husbands, wives, brothers, sisters, and friends losing everything in a matter of seconds. Even after having spent a lot of time there, this is a loss that I cannot comprehend. The pain is unimaginable.

There is a chapter in the book of Isaiah that is one of Megan's favorites. Megan often uses it as a prayer, but when I read the chapter, I believe it is about her. I believe it is about the priest. I believe it is about what happens when a heart is fully awake. The entire chapter of Isaiah 61 reminds me of Megan and the priest and others I have come to know, but I'll only share the first three verses here:

The Spirit of the Sovereign Lord is on me,
    because the Lord has anointed me
    to proclaim good news to the poor.
He has sent me to bind up the broken-
    hearted,
    to proclaim freedom for the captives
    and release from darkness for the
    prisoners,
to proclaim the year of the Lord's favor
    and the day of vengeance of our God,
to comfort all who mourn,
    and provide for those who grieve
    in Zion—
to bestow on them a crown of beauty
    instead of ashes,
the oil of joy
    instead of mourning,
and a garment of praise
    instead of a spirit of despair
    [italics added].
They will be called oaks of righteousness,
    a planting of the Lord
    for the display of his splendor.

There are moments in every life, or sometimes even in entire countries, when we will experience devastation. I believe a significant reason we're meant to live fully awake is that we can bring beauty instead of ashes, joy where there has been mourning, and praise in the place of despair. But if I am not living fully awake, how can I bring what I have not experienced? And this is the reason for love. This is the reason for an awakened heart. There is little we can do to keep our lives clear of tragedy and pain, yet it is our choices that both find and bring beauty into the world.

I believe one of the greatest tragedies on earth is that many who have entered our world have experienced nothing but suffering. Many on this side of heaven have known only misery. I think the reason Jesus commanded us to love our neighbors as ourselves was that we could *be the experience* of beauty, wonder, and magic in the lives of those who need it most.

When we fail to choose to live our lives fully awake, the ashes will extinguish the beauty, the mourning will smother the joy, and the despair will end our praise. When we sleep to the dreams inside our hearts, the message of love will become nothing more than a nice idea. Yet when we awaken to the dreams God has placed inside of us, our very lives become the beauty, magic, and wonder that the world needs.

Megan understands how to find beauty. She knows how to seek out wonder. Yet what is most lovely about Megan is that she doesn't just stop with experiencing beauty; she understands that she is also meant to be the beauty the world needs to see.

Not everyone will be called to go to Haiti, but every life needs to *experience* beauty. It is a large part of the reason we were created. Each time we choose to step into the worlds of our neighbors, to *be the beauty* in their world, we awaken their hearts to the One who *is* love. And every time we choose to love, our hearts are opened wider so that eventually we can look back and see that how we love now is light-years beyond how we loved in the past.

It's not hard to love someone. It's often not even about the size of the act of love; it's about the act itself. Whether it is the simple act of helping someone move, making them dinner, or offering words of encouragement, every act of love is an act of awakening hearts—yours as well as those you have chosen to love. Every act, no matter how small, will draw you closer to God. This is the story we are meant to live, you and I. This is the story that brings beauty instead of ashes, joy where there had been mourning, and praise in the place of despair.

zph.com/awake/9.7

CHAPTER TEN

Patchwork
July 2002 South Africa

It was just after 10:00 p.m., and I was driving home from yet another youth event. I was angry. Megan and I had broken up months earlier, and I had been feeling sorry for myself ever since. I'd been filling my time teaching in high schools and leading youth events at a church. I wasn't enjoying most of it, but to be honest, I was so heartbroken that I wasn't enjoying much of anything. I was angry with Megan, and I was angry with God. In retrospect, I am fully aware that I was pouting like a little child, but at the time I didn't see it that way. I was sure my anger was justified.

I remember that I was also ravenously hungry. I hadn't eaten all day — and it had been a long day. I grabbed my wallet and looked inside. Back then, I could barely afford to put gas in my car, let alone go out to eat. I counted twenty-six Rand, about the equivalent of three dollars and fifty cents. I knew exactly where I was headed.

As I parked my car, five street kids ran up to my door. They looked to be between the ages of seven and twelve and were obviously hungry. All of the kids were extremely skinny, with tattered clothes and hollow eyes. Having lived in South Africa for a couple of years, I was used to the sight. South Africa has a 40 percent unemployment rate, so enormous numbers of homeless men, women, and children walk the streets. Sadly, this fact no longer moved me in the way it should have. My self-absorbed attitude allowed me to completely ignore the kids as I exited my car. They asked for food and money, and I barely looked at them as I pushed my way past and walked straight into McDonald's. I was irritated that these dirty homeless kids were in my way.

I didn't need to look at the menu. I knew exactly what I was going to get: a big-size Big Mac meal with a junior cheeseburger on the side. This would take almost every cent I had left, but I knew the food would bring me some degree of satisfaction. Eating has always been one of my favorite activities in life.

While I was standing in line at McDonald's, God began speaking to me. In the middle of my pity party I suddenly began thinking about the kids outside. I didn't want to, but I think God was whispering to my heart. Sadly, this whispering didn't awaken my heart; instead, it made me even more irritated. I knew God was asking me to feed these kids, but I was hungry, and giving was the last thing in the world I wanted to do. I had just spent my entire weekend preaching and leading worship and ministering, and I couldn't believe that God still wanted more.

By the time the woman behind the counter asked me what I wanted to order, I was all-out angry. The poor lady had to ask three times before I finally answered, the bitterness obvious on my tongue: "Give me five junior hamburgers."

I paid the woman and then waited for the burgers, knowing that I would be going to bed hungry. I didn't say anything to God, and I didn't pray; I simply let my indignation grow.

"I can't believe God wants me to give this all away! Who does he think he is? Doesn't he see what I've been doing?"

I'm ashamed and embarrassed that I was so self-centered. Yet these were the thoughts that flitted across my mind as the woman handed over the bag of burgers. I didn't thank her; I just turned and stalked angrily toward the exit.

It was just after I stepped outside that the miracle happened. Huddled together in the parking lot was a large group of kids. I never counted, but there were definitely more than ten. As I stood there, a bag of burgers in my hand, my heart began to break.

These kids were truly hungry; they may in fact have been starving. As I watched them, I began to feel ridiculous for being so self-absorbed. One child held my gaze. She was a young girl no older than ten. Her face was smudged and dirty, and her gaze was piercing. And this is the moment of the miracle. This is the moment I finally awoke from my long slumber. In an instant, my anger and self-pity faded and was replaced by a deep love for these kids.

I didn't have another penny. There was nothing else I could physically do — the five burgers would be all I could give. I put my hand in the bag and brought out a burger wrapped in yellow paper. As I handed it to the girl, the gratefulness in her eyes was overwhelming. Next, a young boy reached out. As I lifted a burger from the bag, his hand darted in and grabbed it. He immediately began unwrapping it in a rush to get to the food. That's when the chaos started. All of the kids realized I was handing out food, and they became a mob of outstretched hands and loud pleas for help.

By the time my hand went in for the third burger, I began to pray: "Jesus," I muttered, "these kids have nothing. Provide for their needs. God, I'm so sorry. I have so much, and I didn't even see these kids. Please God ..."

I was praying harder than I had in some time. My heart was filled with love for these kids as I continued to hand out the burgers. The whole thing happened in less than a minute. It was only when I handed a burger to the last girl that I realized everyone had been fed. What? All of the kids were sitting or standing around me with grateful looks on their faces and burgers in their hands. I looked inside the bag, and to my amazement I saw a final burger at the very bottom.

I was stunned. I walked over to my car in a daze, got in, and drove away. Over the next few minutes, my heart began to leap in my chest as I started to praise God in a way I had never praised him before. I decided not to drive home. I turned around and drove to my pastor's house. I needed to tell someone what God had done.

As I was driving, God began speaking to my heart.

"This was for you, Joel."

"What do you mean, God?"

"I did this to show my power. I did this to show you that it's not about you."

zph.com/awake/10.1

I was confused. I started thinking about what had actually happened. I had never heard of something like this that wasn't directly attached to some amazing man or woman of God. But God did this amazing thing when I was full of self-pity and anger. I wasn't even talking to him at the time.

He spoke to my heart again. "Joel, I did this to remind you that even at your best you are unusable to me. You could spend your next ten years risking and sacrificing and doing—and still, I would never know you. But when you can live awake to your need of me, you have access to everything I am. Today you were in need of me, and you didn't even know it. When you can start to live from this place, that is where my love is found."

Whenever someone tells me that God told them something or that they witnessed a miracle, my first response is usually skepticism. I don't like this about myself, and I don't think it's healthy, but there it is. Often, when I tell people the story of the McDonald's miracle, I'll see their eyes glaze over a bit as they take a small step back. I'll often be asked questions like, "Do you think that maybe the girl behind the counter gave you too many burgers?" or "Do you think that somebody in the back got the orders wrong, or maybe you took someone else's bag?"

Whatever the question, my usual response is yes. It is quite possible that the lady saw my grumpy demeanor, and—knowing I was one of the last customers for the night—she decided to brighten up my day by giving me the rest of the burgers. It's also possible that someone got the order wrong or the server handed me the wrong bag. The reality is that God often uses people to create his miracles. I also believe it is possible that God actually likes McDonald's enough to multiply their food. In this story, the only thing that mattered was that everyone got a hamburger.

When I was walking into McDonald's, my heart was asleep. Over the previous year, I had chosen to "do the right thing" as I saw it. I worked at the church and spoke at high schools regularly. I told a lot of stories about Jesus and how he wanted a relationship with the students. I told them about the power of an awakened heart and the importance of learning to dream. Yet even as I did these things, I was pouting and angry and didn't have a close relationship with God. I was sleepwalking.

I still went on hikes, and I still embraced risk. I jumped off a building or two, and I skydived regularly. I did my best to love other people and awaken my heart through collecting a bunch of amazing stories. What was different about this year was that each time I would step out and "do it for the story," my heart would awaken slightly, but then it very quickly fell back to sleep again.

What finally woke me from my slumber had nothing to do with the burgers. The moment I realized every kid had something to eat was awesome; but on its own, it wasn't enough to awaken my heart. What woke me from my slumber was the realization of my desperate need.

The street kids had immense need. They had no money, house, parents, school, food—you name it. But even this need wasn't enough; it simply pointed me toward my true need. I don't believe that philanthropy, sacrifice, risk, and courage are enough to keep our hearts awake. I don't think beauty, wonder, magic, and whimsy on their own result in a life well lived. They make great stories, but great stories on their own have little meaning.

The patchwork of my life, the stories I've collected over my past thirty-five years, only has meaning because of Jesus. When I don't live out of my need for God, when my actions aren't based on experiencing him more, my heart will stay asleep. He must be the reason I embrace the story. When I am able to live with a constant revelation of my need for him, even jumping off a building suddenly has deep meaning.

The Sad One

The only thing sadder than a heart that is sleeping is a heart that constantly has to get another story in order to feel alive. God has commanded us all to live the best story possible. He commanded us to love ourselves that much. Yet when we lose sight of the fact that we are living these stories *for* him and *because of* him, our lives quickly lose meaning. Suddenly we find ourselves living for the next big thing or event.

What awakens our heart is no longer the beauty of God but the iPad3, the new film, the next stunt, or the awesome product that just hit the shelves.

zph.com/awake/10.2

And when we buy it, or when we perform the stunt, our hearts are momentarily satisfied. But the satisfaction never lasts. It never comes with new revelation, and it never inspires us to dream. Before we know it, we go back to being sound asleep and feeling empty.

What set apart the extraordinary men, women, and children whose stories wind their way into the Old and New Testaments was not simply the fact that they lived great stories filled with beauty and adventure. Their stories are told thousands of years later because they were people who lived with a constant revelation of their need for God. They are people who fully embraced their story out of their desire to become closer to God.

Cold, Miserable, Awesome

November 2007 Antarctica

Earlier I told a short story about the time I took a boat over to Antarctica. Although I love this story, it doesn't come close to what I experienced the first time I went to the frigid continent. In late 2007, I flew over to Patriot Hills, Antarctica, to film a documentary and miniseries about my good friend Alex Harris. Alex hoped to become the first South African to trek unsupported across that frozen wasteland to the South Pole.

Alex is without a doubt the most insane man I have ever met. He has climbed the seven summits and accomplished countless more amazing feats. Alex is also the reason I thought I was going to die during my first night on the continent.

COLD TO DEATH
"What am I doing here?" I said to the tent "ceiling."

Even the sound of my voice was better than the wind. The wind was constant—fierce and howling like the sound of a ghostly army on the move.

"This has to be the stupidest thing you've ever done, you idiot," I said aloud. And I meant it. I had dreamed about this moment for well over a year, and here I was, just fifteen hours after I had arrived, miserable and afraid.

The real problems were my lightweight sleeping bag and the lack of a mat to place on the tent floor. The cold was seeping through the bag, and my body was beginning to feel numb. I was worried.

I was remembering my conversation with Alex from just a week earlier. We had been standing in his living room in South Africa, waist-deep in gear.

"Do you think I should bring the minus-forty sleeping bag?" I asked.

"It's up to you, really. You're only there for a few weeks. The minus-ten is a little smaller and lighter."

I could tell his mind wasn't on our conversation. Alex was busy going through his own gear, and he didn't have the time to help me pack too. He would be spending close to three months over there, while I was only going for nineteen days.

Trying to look impressive and hard-core, I responded in a very matter-of-fact tone.

zph.com/awake/10.3

"Cool. It'll be nice to have the lighter weight. I don't want a big bag weighing me down while I'm over there."

"Huh?" He wasn't really listening. "Yeah. Sounds good," he said as he shoved his own minus-fifty bag into his rucksack.

I stopped and looked at Alex for a moment. In front of me was a friend who had been on Everest three times, and now I was about to join him on what he considered his "scariest expedition yet." Although I had never done anything even close to this insane, when Alex invited me to accompany him and film his journey, everything he told me set my mind to dreaming and awakened my imagination. There was never a question as to whether or not I would go.

ADVENTURE BREEDS

When we flew into Antarctica, the weather had been perfect. The huge Russian plane (an Ilyushin) had landed on the natural ice runway with ease. We set up camp just sixty-five feet away from several large mess tents that were permanent structures in the base camp. Not twenty minutes after my tent was up, a storm was raging. One minute it was perfect, beautiful, surreal—the next minute it was like something out of a horror film. The exotic and otherworldly landscape had suddenly become a hostile and deadly environment. It was then that I crawled into my tent and opened my bag. I put on every piece of clothing I had and climbed into my minus-ten sleeping bag. For the next five hours, I lay flat on my back, staring at the ceiling, listening to the wind, and growing colder and colder.

"Maybe the mess tents are warmer," I thought as I crawled out of my bag and unzipped the tent. I was immediately blinded by a flurry of snow and ice that coated my goggles. I stood and looked for a moment.

"This is what another planet would be like." This thought popped into my head often during my stay. I had no reference for a place like this.

As I stepped outside my tent, I felt silly for being so afraid. I was still in base camp and only sixty-five feet away from the mess tent. Although it was still desperately cold, and I felt as if the wind might knock me off my feet, I no longer feared getting lost.

To my great pleasure, the inside of the mess tent held relative warmth. An hour later, Alex sauntered in with a small smile curling his lips. He was carrying a few of my belongings. Apparently, the wind had been so fierce that my tent poles had snapped and shredded the tent. Had Alex not been there when it happened, many of my belongings would have blown away. Fortunately for me, he was able to save most of them.

Alex let me know that I had now been initiated into the continent. Although I wasn't seeing the humor, he kept laughing and telling me how funny it was. He then disappeared and came back twenty minutes later with a stronger tent. He told me that the base camp had an ice cave. When I asked, he said

zph.com/awake/10.5

it wasn't "exactly like Superman's." The cave apparently housed a lot of extra tents, mats, and cold-weather gear. I was excited to find that my new tent and floor mats kept my tent at a toasty ten below zero. It was beautiful.

OH, WHAT FUN IT IS TO RIDE

While in Antarctica, I spent a few days on a Ski-Doo shadowing Alex as he trekked through the snow. I went from horizon to horizon, capturing some amazing shots for my documentary.

At one point, my guide and I became lost for thirty-six hours. We were on our Ski-Doos, and we couldn't find Alex's GPS location. A massive storm suddenly descended, the wind blowing more ferociously than I had ever felt before. Unfortunately, the storm broke while we were in the middle of taking down our tent. Without thinking, I pulled out the last stake. Like the sail on a massive ship, the tent blew away with my guide still inside. It rolled and bounced like a huge speeding ball. I had to chase it down, diving with outstretched arms to grab it. My guide was banged up but otherwise OK.

About a week later, I was scheduled to leave Antarctica and fly back to South Africa. I had gotten all the shots I needed, and Alex was going to shoot the rest of the journey on his own. The problem was that the storm was still raging. There was no way to land a plane in the insane winds. Too bored to stay at base camp and unable to leave the continent, I joined some of the base camp staff, and we Ski-Dooed up a giant peak. We brought sleds and skis with us to the top. Not waiting to see which direction we should go, I jumped on my little sled and started down the mountain. I heard someone shout behind me, but it was too late, I couldn't stop, and I couldn't look back. Within seconds, I lost the sled and started tumbling down the thirty-degree, ice-laden slope. The ride was filled with ridges and somersaults, and it ended a full forty seconds later with me desperately digging my feet into the ice to stop myself from running into an outcropping of rocks.

Minutes later, the base camp staff made their way down on their skis in a slow zigzag pattern. They couldn't believe I had taken the sled down that particular slope. They had never done it before because they thought it was too dangerous. After seeing me alive and well, we all made our way back to the top and went down three more times that day.

I played ice hockey on a natural ice runway. I pulled a sled across the wasteland. I hiked up mountains and jumped sastrugi (moguls) on my Ski-Doo. I met extraordinary people and had adventures that would make Hollywood salivate.

When the Credits Roll

I loved my time in Antarctica. I want more of these kinds of stories. I'm excited about discovering more of the dreams that have been hidden in my soul. I think God loves my stories as much as I do. I think he smiled when I jumped from the crane and danced a little jig when I married Megan. I'm guessing God may have laughed out loud when I had to chase down my rolling tent with my guide stuck inside. I believe he was deeply moved when I was serving in Haiti just after the earthquake. I know that it touches God's heart whenever I choose to love my neighbor with my actions.

zph.com/awake/10.6

Yet I think the reason God loves my stories has little to do with the stories themselves. I think he loves them because they have brought me closer to him. Each time I've stepped out and chosen to make God the center of my story, my heart has been awakened to his love.

When we live blind to our need for God, the only place we think we'll find him is in church on a Sunday morning or in the Bible when we take the time to read it. And though I believe these things can be absolutely critical to our relationship with God, on their own, I think they lead only to a shallow recognition of his existence. They lead to a religion that is more concerned with appearance than the heart. And they lead to a people who are more concerned with sin than with love.

But when we are aware of our need for God, there is suddenly no distinction between sacred and secular. When we keep our need constantly before us, God will be found in the midst of the story. He will be experienced at the bottom of the crane or in that samba lesson you've been too embarrassed to take. He will be waiting on the other side of your decision to run after the one you love. He will suddenly be at the center of that crazy idea you just can't shake. He will be experienced when we choose to love with our actions.

I don't want to live sound asleep and feeling empty. I want my life to be messy and chaotic and filled with unexpected beauty and moments of wonder. I want to experience the God of the Bible here and now, not simply to learn about him there and then. Jesus actually told us that our lives are meant to be more magical than any that came before, including his own. He implied that our lives should be filled with miracles and wonder: "Very truly I tell you, whoever believes in me will do the works I have been doing, and they will do even greater things than these" (John 14:12).

God has commanded us to be his hands and feet. He wants us to *show* him to the world, not just *tell* him to the world. He told us to heal those who need healing, to bind up the brokenhearted, and to bring justice to the oppressed. But we cannot do these things unless every aspect of our lives is about drawing us closer to him.

Just this morning I was reading from Hebrews 11:

By faith we understand . . .

By faith Enoch . . . did not experience death . . .

By faith Noah . . . built an ark . . .

By faith Abraham . . . went, even though he did not know where he was going . . . And by faith even Sarah . . . was enabled to bear children . . .

By faith Joseph . . . spoke . . .

By faith Moses' parents hid him . . .

By faith Moses . . . persevered because he saw him who is invisible . . .

By faith the prostitute Rahab . . . welcomed the spies . . .

Through faith [many people of God] conquered kingdoms, administered justice, . . . shut the mouths of lions, . . . escaped the edge of the sword . . .

It is easy to read this chapter and be blown away by stuff like Enoch not experiencing death and the mouths of lions being miraculously closed. But as I've begun to see the whole story, I've come to realize that just as many "everyday miracles" are mentioned in this great chapter as there are "extraordinary miracles": building, traveling, speaking, hiding, persevering, welcoming, and administering justice. Just as there is no dividing line between secular and sacred, there is no distinction between epic adventures and ordinary living. All that matters is whether or not we keep God at the center of our stories.

Scan QR code and place
device here or go to
zph.com/awake/10.7

When we understand that Christ is the center of all we do, being a priest is a godly thing, but so is being a filmmaker or the guy who designs tents to withstand Antarctic winds or a stay-at-home mother. Handing out water and blankets brings glory to God, but so does making cheeseburgers. When we act out of our need for God, the seemingly ordinary becomes the miraculous, and the seemingly mundane becomes the magical.

I believe that our stories, yours and mine, are meant to rival those that came before. Our invitation is to keep the story line moving, turning the page into each new adventure God has for us, each opportunity to love God more deeply, love others more strongly, and love ourselves more fully.

I pray these pages will inspire you to find God in the midst of your story, to learn what awakens your soul, and to embrace every dream God has given you.

The Beginning

ACKNOWLEDGMENTS

First and foremost, I must thank the wife of my youth, my snuggler of note, the woman who holds my heart in the palm of her hand. Thank you, my love, for encouraging me to write this and for finally saying yes. Megan Nykyforchyn-Clark, from the moment I met you, my heart was awakened and my world was transformed. I love you.

I must thank my two biggest heroes, my mom and dad. Your lives have inspired all of your children to pursue God with all of our hearts, to be willing to risk no matter the stakes, and to be ridiculously good-looking. Mom, I thank you for that last part most of all. To my brother, Jason, you are my favorite writer and the best brother in the world. Your constant encouragement and belief in me mean more than I could ever tell you. To my sister and hero, Aimee, you are my favorite dreamer, and you have consistently pointed me toward God in virtually every conversation we have ever had. You amaze me. To Josiah and Ben, the two true artists in the family, I am so excited to see where your passions take you and what comes of your dreams. I love you guys.

To the two people who most made this book come alive, Mike Cody and Heidi Tungseth—Mike, your artwork is simply amazing. You took my stories and turned them into so much more. I will be pitching you as artist extraordinaire for years to come and calling you often for more brilliance, I am sure. Heidi, it's amazing to see where a random coffee can lead. Thank you for adding to the experience of this book. I trust we will continue to work together in the future!

Nicholas Costaras, you are the best business partner

zph.com/awake/ak1

and friend one could hope for. It was God who put us together. The journey has been amazing thus far, and I cannot wait to see where it leads. That said, I could go my whole life without sharing a bed with you in a lovetell ever again.

Truck Stop (aka Mike Albert), your edits and encouragements have meant the world. We must sit in a tub in Haiti in our boxers with a beer in our hands again soon. Your book is next, my friend. You are the master writer among us.

Bill and Deb, you have always amazed me. Thank you, first of all, for creating Megan—great job on that! Thank you, secondly, for your constant encouragement.

Father Richard Frechette (aka The Priest), every moment I have spent with you has both challenged me to be more and inspired me to love more. My dream in life is to be more like you.

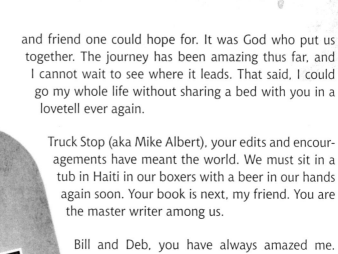

zph.com/awake/ak2

Mark Batterson, thanks for believing in me, as well as being willing to offer your constant encouragement and help me get connected. Kasey Kirby and Bryan John-Phillip van Niekerk, it was a party in Antarctica; let's make something even crazier next time.

Douard Le Roux, it's been too long since I've had the opportunity to jump off something or break any laws. When are we getting together again? Wisner Liberté and Jean Marc Zamor, you are both an inspiration to me. Your friendship means the world. Though we have not connected lately, I know our paths will continue to cross. I cannot wait until next we meet.

Kali Nanayeo Ajiman Ilunga, your inogulence knows no bounds. You are one of the most brilliant men I've ever met. I am honored to know you and call you a friend. Thanks for the review (wink, wink). Whenever you start to feel too good about yourself, just remember what happened when you touched my car radio one too many times.

Gareth Moore, though we no longer live near each other, you are one of my closest friends. You are a true storyteller. Let's smoke a cigar together soon. Ekkehart Hoening, you were pivotal in more than one story in this book. Due to length constraints you were taken out, but know that I understand just how much you impacted my life.

Jonathan Lee, though I know you will continue to grow in wisdom and stature, I pray you never make the mistake of growing up. Thank you for the laughs and the "random" jokes. Alex Harris, let's go get a massive breakfast sometime soon. I miss those times! Shall we cross the Empty Quarter next?

Bill and Connie Bennot, though you are never mentioned by name in this book, you are the reason for much of it. You are my pastors, and I crave your wisdom. Thank you for the years of encouragement and believing in me.

Jason and Tricia Treadwell, Amy Coop Wiederwohl, Sandy Alva, and Jeff Tew, your friendship back in 1995 and through the years has meant a lot. Jason, I must fall asleep on your hairy chest again soon.

Esther Fedorkevich, what can I say? Wow. You made this happen. Thanks for getting behind this project in such a personal way. You gave it everything. Thank you.

zph.com/awake/ak3

Lee Hough, you believed in me when no one else did. Thank you for believing.

John Blase, you helped me focus and tweak in a way that only a master of this craft could do. You have a cool name as well. Andy Meisenheimer, thanks for pushing me hard, even when I didn't like you for it.

And last but certainly not least, Carolyn McCready, thank you for sticking your neck on the line and bringing me out to Grand Rapids. Thanks for your edits. I know this won't be the last project we work on together. Verne Kenney, Andrea Lyons, Don Gates, Tom Dean, Dirk Buursma, Cindy Lambert, Sarah Johnson, Jacob Noorman, Merideth Bliss, and the rest of the team at Zondervan, who worked tirelessly, pulling out all the stops to make this book an amazing experience, thank you from the bottom and top of my heart!

zph.com/awake/ak4

ABOUT JOEL NYKYFORCHYN-CLARK

Joel Nykyforchyn-Clark is the cofounder and president of Switchvert, an ideas/ film production house co-located in Washington, D.C., and Johannesburg, South Africa (www.switchvert .com). Since he was a child, Clark has been captivated by storytelling—and his journey has been influenced by a deep desire to witness and tell stories that challenge paradigms. A captivating raconteur, Clark has written and directed documentaries, films, commercials, and short stories covering topics ranging from child slavery in Haiti to an Antarctic sitcom. Convinced that all great stories lead toward God, whether they are spoken, written, or filmed, Clark weaves a beautiful mosaic he hopes will draw observers into deeper intimacy with their creator. Clark lives with his wife of six years, Megan, in Washington, D.C.

Check out Clark's blog at www.joelnclark.com.

Check out his company at www.switchvert.com.

So you thought the book was done, didn't you?

You thought the story was over. But that's just silly; story never ends. My amazing editor, Carolyn McCready, asked me if I had any parting thoughts for you, the reader. Here I sit, three months before this book hits the shelves, and she wanted to know if there was anything "burning inside me."

The answer is yes.

I wrote a blog entry recently I want to share with you. I have reproduced it below. By the way, you can check out my blog at www.joelnclark.com.

Throughout the process of writing *Awake*, I have learned more about God and about myself than I've learned through anything I've ever done before. Although I've collected many unbelievable stories in my short thirty-five years on earth, I hadn't really taken the time to learn from them. The tapestry of God's love—his hand and his faithfulness in my life—was not immediately obvious.

Only when I sat down and wrote these stories out did I clearly see God's hand at work. Only then did I hear his voice. Almost every revelation I've had was not an actual "revelation" until I had taken the time to think through it and write it down. I have crashed through much of my life seeking the next adventure, the next story, without ever stopping to learn from them.

I strongly encourage you to write out your stories. If we take the time to decipher what God has been teaching us through them, we will find him in the midst of every single story. I am convinced of it.

A friend of mine recently berated me for my "do it for the story" message. He told me it was "irrelevant." He said, "When I change my one-year-old's diaper, I am not doing it for the story; I am simply changing a diaper. Everything is not story."

But I couldn't disagree more. I don't think it's the size of the story that matters. We will all experience magic and pain, the wild and the mundane. Megan and I are expecting our first child just a few days after this book releases. And I will change my baby's diaper "for the story" because I now understand that God is in the midst of the mundane and the silly and the supposedly meaningless. I now understand that I will find him in the midst of EVERY story, and I now know there is no such thing as "meaningless." For this is what life is about—finding God.

I no longer doubt whether God is speaking to me. The question is, "Am I listening?" If I am, I will hear him, and it is impossible to hear God without experiencing transformation. And in the coming months, I plan to change many diapers for the story. This is my burning message. This is my story.

Share Your Thoughts

With the Author: Your comments will be forwarded to the author when you send them to *zauthor@zondervan.com*.

With Zondervan: Submit your review of this book by writing to *zreview@zondervan.com*.

Free Online Resources at
www.zondervan.com

Zondervan AuthorTracker: Be notified whenever your favorite authors publish new books, go on tour, or post an update about what's happening in their lives at www.zondervan.com/authortracker.

Daily Bible Verses and Devotions: Enrich your life with daily Bible verses or devotions that help you start every morning focused on God. Visit www.zondervan.com/newsletters.

Free Email Publications: Sign up for newsletters on Christian living, academic resources, church ministry, fiction, children's resources, and more. Visit www.zondervan.com/newsletters.

Zondervan Bible Search: Find and compare Bible passages in a variety of translations at www.zondervanbiblesearch.com.

Other Benefits: Register to receive online benefits like coupons and special offers, or to participate in research.

ZONDERVAN®

ZONDERVAN.com/
AUTHORTRACKER
follow your favorite authors